Cliff Parker has been described as Angling's
Number One Humorist. As he's often been called
worse, he's prepared to settle for it.

Born in Manchester so as to be near his parents,
Parker was eventually moved on by the Keep
Britain Tidy people and now lives in Amersham,
Bucks, with wife, two children, insane cat and
permanent overdraft.

Hobbies are fishing, frog fancying and working
towards sainthood. Ambition is to be locked in a
pub with Brigitte Bardot. Reports that Miss
Bardot's ambition is to be locked in a pub with
Cliff Parker have yet to be confirmed.

FISHING FOR LAFFS is just that: a collection
of Parker's funniest fishing stories, originally
published in the specialist angling press.

D1555809

Also by Cliff Parker in Sphere Books:

THE COMPLEAT WALLY ANGLER
THE FISHING HANDBOOK TO END ALL
   FISHING HANDBOOKS
HOOK, LINE AND STINKER
SLING YOUR HOOK

Fishing For Laffs

CLIFF PARKER

SPHERE BOOKS LIMITED
London and Sydney

First published in Great Britain by
Sphere Books Ltd 1985
30–32 Gray's Inn Road, London, WC1X 8JL
Copyright © 1985 by Cliff Parker
Cartoons © 1985 by Graham Allen

TRADE
MARK

This book is sold subject to the condition that
it shall not, by way of trade or otherwise, be lent,
re-sold, hired out or otherwise circulated without
the publisher's prior consent in any form of
binding or cover other than that in which it is
published and without a similar condition
including this condition being imposed on the
subsequent purchaser.

Set in Century

Printed and bound in Great Britain by
Cox & Wyman Ltd, Reading

Contents

Fishing For Laffs

1

Animal Crackers

Cousin Jim from Leeds doesn't have much luck with animals. I have mentioned in earlier volumes the cow which fell on him and the horse which towed him down to the river at a speed which made him doubt whether his eyes would ever stop watering. That kind of thing keeps happening to Jim.

We were on the bank one day when his basket started bucking under him.

'This may sound a silly question, our Clifford,' he said, 'but is the bank moving under you?'

'No,' I said. 'In fact it hasn't done since that last session on Mad Mac's home brew.'

'Well it's moving under me,' he said. 'You don't think it's an earthquake?'

'Bit localised for an earthquake,' I said. 'Can't be anything serious. Possibly just a landslip or the beginnings of a small avalanche.'

'Ooh, 'eck,' said Jim. 'What do you reckon I should do?'

My million-dollar brain acted at lightning speed.

'Move,' I said.

Jim took wise old Cousin Clifford's advice and lifted his basket. And there was the cause: a swiftly-rising molehill, being raised, from the look of it, by some new breed of supermole.

He moved the basket along the bank, relieved that it was only a mole and thankful that it hadn't had time to burrow up his trouser leg.

'I don't know what it is with me and animals,' he said. 'But I'm still twitching after that night fishing we did on the Swale.'

1

Me too, if the truth be told. That night had been a bit hair-raising.

We'd gone into the pasture leading down to the river after dark. Jim was leading the way with a torch. Suddenly there was a noise like thunder.

'Storm brewing,' I said. 'Bound to happen to us two.'

But the funny thing was that there was no lightning. Even though the thundering sound was getting closer.

'Eek!' screamed Jim.

Gleaming in the torchlight were a hundred eyes, set in big hairy faces. The thundering had stopped. In its place was the sound of a lot of snorting and heavy breathing; we were surrounded by a herd of bullocks. Attracted by the torchlight, they'd stampeded towards us from all corners of the field.

Jim turned the torch off. 'It's all right now, our Clifford,' he said. 'They'll go away. Just keep close and we'll – Oof!'

They hadn't gone away yet. Jim had walked straight into a bullock which was much bigger than he was.

We stood there for a bit, making cowboy noises, and then risked the rest of the walk to the bank, flashing the torch only now and again to give us our bearings.

'This is the life,' said Jim a bit later as we sat back and waited for bites. 'Peace and ... just a minute ... there's a train coming.'

'Probably a milk train at this time,' I said. 'Funny though, it sounds like a steam train.'

'Steam train or not,' said Jim. 'This place doesn't even have a station.'

'Eek!'

The sound seemed now to be directly behind us and not very far away.

Chuff-chuff . . . chuff-chuff . . . chuff-chuff . . .

Jim turned round and shone the torch. And there was the chuffer – a blinking and very bewildered hedgehog.

'Chuff off,' said Jim. And off it chuffed.

Peace reigned again, as they say. The only sounds were the lapping of the water and the odd slurp as Jim and I took turns with the Scotch.

Then there was a slight scraping sound behind us and a *cough*. A horrible, dry, rasping cough, like that of some evil old man.

'Who's that?' called Jim.

3

No answer. Except for another harsh and nasty cough.

'Hey up,' said Jim. 'You shine the torch this time.'

'No fear,' I said. 'Didn't you notice as we came in? The graveyard's just over there. Might be one of the old lads on walkabout. Remember that Dracula film on telly the other...'

'Aaargh!' croaked Jim. 'Shurrup!'

But, brave lad that he is, he grabbed the torch and shone it in the direction of the noise.

'Hak hak! Bleargh!' coughed the grumpy old sheep caught in the glare.

'I've had enough of this,' said Jim, fumbling for the Scotch. 'I'm going to get wellied.'

'After you, Cousin,' I said.

Which is why, as the sun rose slowly over the Swale, it was greeted by the sight of two weary, bleary and well-wellied anglers, raising their voices in comforting song:

> *All things bright and beautiful,*
> *All creatures great and...*

'All right, our Jim?'

'I am now, our Clifford. Don't be too long with that bottle...'

2

Sex and the Single Angler

Uncle Clifford's Worry Corner, angling's answer to Marjorie Proops, has received a moving letter from a lonely angler in Rock Ferry, Merseyside.

Tom is a dedicated fisherman, out weekends and evenings in all weathers, and he's getting the sneaking feeling that he might be missing something, i.e. wimmin.

He used to be married but apparently his missis showed him the yellow card once or twice about the time he spent on the bank. Finally, she confronted him there with a 'Fish-or-Me' ultimatum. Tom was into a hot spot at the time, so that was that.

'Mind you,' writes Tom, 'I did get a cracking bag of roach.'

Which just goes to show that every cloud, etc.

Since then, however, when the fishing hasn't been too clever, Tom's thoughts have strayed to what anglers' thoughts usually stray to at such times.

'Where are all the lovely female fishermen?' he asks.

(Shouldn't that be female fisherpersons, or summat?)

'I've tried finding one,' he says, 'but the nearest I got was while I was fishing the Leeds-Liverpool Canal.'

Now there's a romantic spot if ever there was one – the Leeds-Liverpool Canal. Swaying palms, scented tropical breezes, the sound of distant waves lapping the Mersey shore... Bloody 'ell.

However, our Tom got to chatting up a lady person and things could have led to a whirlwind and tempestuous-type romance. But when the silver-tongued devil compared her beauty to that of a nice tench he'd just caught, somehow the

5

fires of passion were cooled. With a reply which Tom cannot bring himself to commit to print, the lady person was away like the clappers up the towpath. Ne'er to return, as they say.

'So how about,' asks Tom, 'a pen pal column for us poor, shy, rejected anglers?'

Actually, Tom, the Personal Column in the classified ads of angling magazines already caters for such contacts. Or, if you're not in mint condition, there's always the Swap Shop.

But that's only the beginning. You've got to put yourself out a bit if you really want to impress the girls.

Take the advertisement for a start. You've got to sell yourself. To hell with the truth. It's no use putting in an ad which says, 'Middle-aged, scruffy, toothless angler (interests fishing, supping and the other) wishes to meet swinging 19-year-old chick with view to.'

No chance. Phrase it something like, 'Mature outdoor type, of characterful appearance and with preference for casual attire (interests angling, convivial company and meaningful relationships) wishes to meet sympathetic and understanding young lady.' Leave the 'with view to' bit until later. Let it come as a surprise.

Don't be too ambitious. Rich and beautiful sex kittens with a taste for draught bitter might be every angler's dream of home, but there are very few of them not spoken for. First impressions are all-important, so don't arrange a meeting on the bank when you're likely to be in the thick of things and covered in gunje. Arrange it in a pub near the water so that if she screams and rushes immediately out of your life, the evening won't have been entirely wasted. Give your anorak a good scrape down, shine up your wellies and brush the lugs out of your bobbly hat. Comb your hair, or polish your head, and put your teeth in.

Make the trysting place the saloon bar, for once, and choose a seat in a dimly-lit corner. Not only is the soft lighting more romantic, it stops her from examining you too closely. Show her you know how to treat a lady. Spare no expense; let her have a cherry on the top of her stout if she wants to, and as many salt and vinegar crisps as she can eat.

Keep the conversation light and scintillating. And build up your image – the rugged outdoor man, braving the elements and outwitting Nature's fiercest denizens of the deep, goes down a lot better than a blow-by-blow account of how you pulled in half a dozen gudgeon last week. Crack on you're a pike or zander specialist. The image of the intrepid hunter of freshwater sharks is more likely to set a feminine heart-a-flutter than that of a sedentary bream-basher or tiddler-snatcher.

Towards the end of the evening you may detect the occasional seductive yawn from your companion. Does this mean that she's in the mood for a nightcap at your place or hers? Or does it mean that she's bored out of her mind?

It's no use asking me. By this time you are beyond the reach of Uncle Clifford's guiding hand and worldly wisdom. From now on you're on your own.

And the best of British luck...

3

Mind How You Go

Some Good News and some Bad News.

The Good News is that angling makes you look younger and live longer. Several surveys have confirmed that fishing helps towards relaxation and mental health, peace of mind, and all that. Findings such as these always come as a surprise to those of us who at the end of the day are twitching wrecks and who finish the season totally bonkers, but that's the official verdict.

The Bad News, from the Office of Population Census and Surveys, is that angling can seriously damage your health by rendering you dead. Their latest report announces that, in 1982, angling killed more people in Britain than any other single sport or leisure activity. Eleven of us went to the Great Match Peg in the sky, ten by drowning.

The Good News is that it's not nearly as bad as it sounds. Nothing like. There are more anglers out every weekend than those involved in all the other participant sports put together, so it's really a lot safer than soccer, rugger, hang-gliding or attempts at the ferrets-down-the-trousers record.

The Bad News is that there are many more ways of doing yourself a mischief out fishing than are covered in the report, some of which may not be apparent until later. And you ought to be aware of these if you're proposing to get with the relaxation and peace of mind.

For a start, there are always a few heart attacks brought on by the excitement of playing a whopper. I thought my own number was up when, after weeks of trying, I finally netted that big perch. OK, a half-pounder, but on the Grand Union, everything's relative. If it hadn't been for Mad Mac and Big McGinty coming swiftly to my aid with a few swigs of the hard stuff, I may well have passed on through palpitations and tremblement. But what was more dangerous was the secondary shock at the realisation that I'd actually got a drink out of those two.

Heart attacks can be triggered off by other circumstances, such as sprinting fully laden with gear to get to the pub before it shuts. You get there all right, but are in no fit state to sup your ale on account of dropping dead. You can behave sensibly and walk to the pub at a leisurely and even pace. But then you run the risk of arriving just as time is being called; another circumstance likely to do you no good at all.

Secondly, exposure is always a risk in the cold weather. A recent medical theory is that wind can be a shock to the systems of people who are not used to it. (Blowing-type wind, that is. Not the 'Urrrp! Pardon!' kind.) Townies exposed to a good hard blow can suffer from over-stimulation of the doodahs and flake out later on. So reservoir fishers, beware. It's one thing to come home minus your nose or with your ears blown back-to-front, but it's quite another to greet the wife with, 'Evenin', Pet. Where's me tea? It's freezing out... Aaargh!'

Exposure afflicts many anglers whose wives refuse to let them in when they arrive home at two in the morning, singing naughty songs and falling about.

There's nothing for it then but to kip on the lawn, or at best take shelter in the shed for the night. Even the best of sheds gets very cold in the early hours – so I understand – and unless you've got something left in the Scotch bottle, severe hypothermia can set in.

Every year, too, there are many cases of angler-battering. Sometimes the injuries are the result of anti-social actions on the part of the angler, such as pinching somebody else's pre-baited swim, lobbing shampoo sachets into a rival's pitch, or indulging in a few double entries at the weigh-in.

Other injuries are the result of small domestic misunderstandings, such as occur when the angler is left propped up against the front door by cowardly mates who have rung the bell and run away. The angler may do himself a mischief when he falls flat on his face as his wife opens the door. Whether or not, he is still liable to cop for

some corrective therapy, such as being belaboured un-
mercifully with a blunt instrument as he lies helpless and
unconscious on the hall carpet.

There is the occasional case of alcohol poisoning, which
can be brought about because the angler has won the
match and is celebrating his great victory, or because he
has lost the match and is trying to kill the pain, or just
because he likes the stuff. You don't need an excuse,
dammit.

Damage is done every year to anglers incautious enough
to assume that farm animals are harmless, even wandering cheerfully through a field containing a bull. Anybody
shortsighted or gormless enough not to recognise a bull
ought to stick to safer pursuits such as origami or ludo.

A mate of mine was bitten by a pig and contracted swine
fever, which is very serious and nothing to laff about at all.
I tried hard to remember this when I went to see him in
hospital but I was still told off by matron for doing
farmyard imitations detrimental to the patient's peace of
mind.

Another mate was bitten by a sheep and contracted the
rare disease known as Orf. I kid you not. It got its name
perhaps because the disease is so rare that medical
specialists try to keep bits of you for further study. 'Bitten
there, was he? Right. Let's have it orf...'

Finally, there are the casualties brought about by
Tempting Fate. It is all too common for an angler
challenged in the middle of a gigantic fib, or caught doing
naughty things around the scale basket at the weigh-in, to
lay his hand on his heart and declare; 'If I'm not telling the
truth, may the Good Lord strike me down.' The sudden
flash of lightning out of a clear blue sky may restore
people's faith in The Almighty. But it messes up the
statistics no end, as well as playing hell with your peace of
mind.

4

What's Up, Doc?

'I'll have to lose some weight,' said Doc Thumper. 'Sitting on this basket all day is not good for me. It's given me a Condition.'

'Gad!' I expostulated. 'Not...? Not the...? Not the dreaded... *Basket Bum*?'

'Would that it were,' said Doc, lapsing into Shakespeare. 'At least Basket Bum disappears after a few hours. No, this is something much more serious, this is – or these are – [blush blush] *spots*.'

'You ought to see a doctor,' I said.

'Curses!' said Doc, marvelling at my cutting-through mind. 'Why didn't I think of that?'

What Doc had was the dreaded angler's curse – or one of the worst of them – the dreadfully dreaded *Spotty Botty*, brought about by long hours of sitting on wicker baskets and bar stools. Spotty Botty often goes hand in hand, even cheek by jowl, with Basket Bum, which means it can go unnoticed until the impression of the wicker basket on one's botty has faded, and so perhaps escape detection until it turns into something worse.

Funny how different sports have their own particular ailments; a leading British skin specialist discovered that physical activities can cause crops of spots on different parts of the body, brought about by changes in environment and friction on the skin.

Tennis players wearing headbands, for instance, can get 'hippy' acne of the forehead. Swimmers can get poorly earholes through regular overdoses of chlorine. Lady person ball game players often get spots where their bras

11

rub the skin. (The one sure cure for this, apparently, is to play topless. That might do wonders for the Wimbledon telly ratings, but it could cause problems with the forehand volleys.)

Now Spotty Botty can join the list of sporting ailments, along with other afflictions that angling is heir to. Some of the latest, discovered by the Parker Institute for the Study of Anglers' Nasties, are:

Tiddler Snatcher's Tilt. This is caused by carrying a basket and holdall on the right shoulder and a bag of groundbait, brolly and folding stool in the left hand. It results in the right shoulder being hitched up to the earlobe, the left shoulder dropping down to the navel, and the left leg finishing up six inches shorter than the right. The net effect is to give a list to port which carries no ill effects so long as the angler is loaded down with gear. When he drops it, however, he tends to stump around on the spot in anti-clockwise circles; a grave disadvantage when you're trying to reach the pub.

Bream Basher's Belly Button is caused by the angler resting the butt of the rod in his navel. Over the years the navel gets deeper and deeper, until in the end only the reel prevents the butt from coming out the other side. In severe cases, the use of a bath plug is recommended between outings to prevent an undue accumulation of fluff.

The condition can be alleviated a little by inserting a screwdriver into the navel and turning gently anti-clockwise. Do not make too many turns if you do not wish your bum to fall off.

Wader's Wobblies are caused by the friction of wader tops, and are particularly severe in the case of a short angler wearing tall waders. Symptoms, apart from a funny walk, are watering eyes and a pained expression.

One of these days, as more and more hatchback cars are used, another condition might join the list: *Headlessness*. (Makes a change from *Leglessness*.)

Hatchbacks are popular among anglers because there's plenty of room for tackle and it's easy to get the stuff in and out. My mate Mitch bought one and he went fishing with his mate Fred from the allotments. After the session, Mitch drove back to Fred's place, parked in the drive, and lifted up the hatch for Fred to take his gear out. Out it came, and

Mitch got hold of the handle and slammed down the hatch. Unfortunately, Fred had just spotted something he'd left behind and poked his head back into the car.

BOINGGG! went the hatch, hard down on the back of Fred's head. The poor bloke staggered away, bent double, clutching his head and groaning, 'The Bells! The Bells...!'

Out came Missis Fred.

'Hello, Mitch,' she said. 'Catch anything?'

'Not a lot,' said Mitch. 'Half a dozen roach and a one-eyed perch.'

'How's Dolly,' asked Missis Fred. 'And young Daniel?'

'They're fine, thanks,' said Mitch. 'And you? Keeping well?'

'Can't grumble,' said Missis Fred.

Just then Fred came staggering back after a tour of the garden, still bent double, clutching his head and groaning, 'The Bells! The Bells...!'

'What's the matter with Fred?' said Missis Fred. 'All that stuff about The Bells. You've not had him on the Scotch again?'

'No,' said Mitch. 'He's just had a small mishap with my new motor car. Thinks he's the Hatchback of Notre Dame...'

5

Match Loser's Talkin' Blues

There are few times more depressing for anglers than when the coarse season draws to its close and the matches are over for three whole months, but at least the close season saves a lot of lads from assaults upon their persons and cloggings behind the clubhouse.

Statistics prove that most matches are won by one team and lost by another. (I didn't get where I am today without knowing that.)

And for every team that loses, there's generally some poor lad who gets the blame. Sometimes two or three of them, which is the occasion for a double or triple duffing. I know how they feel, being a past master at lowering the team weight.

This is the stuff that sad songs are made of. And as some kind of consolation to these unfortunate lads, I have composed a little song entitled *Match Loser's Talkin' Blues*. It is based on the blues style of the great Howlin' Wolf, and comes to you now by courtesy of Caterwaulin' Cliff:

MATCH LOSER'S TALKIN' BLUES

I woke up this mornin'
Wishin' I was dead.

Yes, I woke up this mornin'
Wishin' I was dead.

'Cos I lost the team the aggregate
An' they broke the scales on my head.

(All right you lot laffin'. Bloody painful, that is.)

I woke up this mornin'
Feelin' so uptight.

Yes, I woke up this mornin'
Feelin' so uptight.

'Cos they sat me on a pile o' dud bettin' slips
An' somebody struck a light.

(Yes, they really put me in the hot seat. I'll never enjoy
Guy Fawkes Night again.)

I woke up this mornin'
Feelin' very low.

I woke up this mornin'
Feelin' very low.

'Cos the wife had upped an' left me
An' taken the kids in tow.

(And the cat had whoopsied on the carpet, the budgie
had caught psittacosis and the hamster had dropped
down dead. Not bad for starters.)

I woke up this mornin'
Feelin' kind o' rum.

Yes, I woke up this mornin'
Feelin' kind o' rum.

There were thirty five rod rests through my head
An' twelve more stuck in my bum.

(I can't tell you where the other seventy three went. Kof
kof. Ooh, me chest...)

I woke up this mornin'
Feelin' kind o' sick.

Yes, I woke up this mornin'
Feelin' kind o' sick.

'Cos the lads had hired a hit man
And he hit me with a brick.

(A good quality textured outdoor brick, mind you. Not
one of your cheap old stock bricks for inside jobs.
Which showed a bit of consideration.)

I woke up this mornin'
Feelin' kind o' sad.

Yes, I woke up this mornin'
Feelin' kind o' sad.

'Cos the feller with the brick who hit me
Turned out to be my dad.

(Sayin', 'After what you done you ain't no son o' mine,
boy. An' how come you got the milkman's nose
anyway?'
Nobody's perfect, I always say.)

I woke up this mornin'
An' I was dyin' o' thirst.

Yes, I woke up this mornin'
An' I was dyin' o' thirst.

But I got thrown out of the boozer
'Cos the landlord thought the worst.

(Thought it was me blew the match. Hadn't heard about the duff peg, contrary winds, biased stewards and crooked match secretaries. Silly person.)

I woke up this mornin'
Feelin' left in the lurch.

Yes, I woke up this mornin'
Feelin' left in the lurch.

So I went to see the vicar
But he'd just pawned the church.

('All on account o' you, you no good, no 'count, dozy angler, you. And it was you who recommended the bookie if I remember rightly. Aa-aah-men...')

I woke up this mornin'
Badly hit by the lousies

Yes, I woke up this mornin'
Badly hit by the lousies.

'Cos they'd stuffed a dead bream up my jumper
And a live pike down my trousies.

(And if you think that's funny you should try it some time. With them backward-pointing teeth, nothing that goes in ever comes out...)

I woke up this mornin'
Feelin' very blue.

Yes, I woke up this mornin'
Feelin' very blue.

'Cos they'd stitched up my flies with eight-pound line
And filled my Y-fronts up with glue.

(Soopergloo. Sets in a second. Get out of that...)

I woke up this mornin'
Feelin' iller an' iller.

Yes, I woke up this mornin'
Feelin' iller an' iller

'Cos they'd gone an' filled my wellies
With a stone of Polyfilla.

(And then chucked me in the cut. It's awful cold
and wet in there. Oh, lawdy, lawdy. Gurgle gurgle...)

I

  Need

    A

      Friend ...

6

All in the Game

Amazing, the number of video games there are about. You can fight space aliens, avoid asteroids, zap enemy spaceships, intercept ballistic missiles, knock hell out of destructive mutants and even gobble up ghosts. It's all a bit too violent for me; I'm more your ludo man or tiddlywinks person.

One video game, popular in Japan, has been banned from Britain on the grounds of taste. On the screen you have a burning building, from which babies are dropping. You have to catch each baby before it hits the ground – otherwise it explodes and a little angel floats to the top of the screen. Dunno, it doesn't seem any less tasteful than all that zapping and gobbling and crunching and lasering. At least you try to stop the poor little mites exploding. Presumably if they were space alien babies and you were zapping them to save your planet, there'd be no problems.

Sales of video games are booming month by month, and it's hard to get into a pub these days without having to climb over a bunch of Youthful Operators Ballistics (YOBs for short) clustered around a machine. (Ee, you're getting real crusty in your old age, Parker.)

'Good for them,' say the manufacturers. 'By playing our machines they will improve on almost everything. They will become mathematical geniuses, be able to fly a jet plane, whizz round Brands Hatch with their eyes closed and perhaps do the odd bit of brain surgery in their lunch hours.' But what is there for those of us who do not wish to become a mathematical genius or whatever, who do not want to zap or splat anything, but who would like to improve our fishing? Where are the angling video games? I'll tell you where, brothers. Nowhere, that's where.

Until now.

To the rescue, as usual, has come the Parker Million-Dollar Brain (patent applied for), with a range of video games for the discerning angler. Improve your techniques up to world standard within seconds. All right, then, minutes. All you need are Superman reflexes and a sack of 50p pieces. Ready?

Whoopsie. Cross the field down to the bank without stepping into a cowpat. Step into one and you can only move diagonally. Step into two and you walk round in circles. Step into three and you explode. (Sorry about that, but if you step into three you deserve to explode.)

Bullseye. Make your way through a herd of cows without getting close enough to upset any of them. One of them is bound to be upset, whatever you do, because it's a bull. Can you leap the stile before the bull gives you a helping horn?

Walk the bank. You are walking along the top of a river bank, carefully avoiding all the crumbly bits. Somewhere is a bit which looks safe, but which is undercut. Only careful testing can reveal which – but here comes that bull again...

What's this ear? You are casting into a strong side wind, which keeps taking your hook close to the ear of the bloke next to you. He's sitting far too close, but he weighs 16 stone and has a broken nose, so you don't really like to tell him. Can you keep your hook out of his ear? If not, can you escape the ham-sized fist which is speeding in the direction of your own little shell-like?

Two fingers. You are unhooking a pike without a gag. Can you get the hook out within five seconds? Or must your pianoforte technique and nose picking be ruined for ever?

With friends like these... You are sitting in a pub after the match, with the price of only two more pints in your pocket. In walk Mad Mac and Big McGinty, both of whom you know are skint. Can you crawl under the tables and out of the back door without being spotted?

...Who needs enemies? You did mean to get your ticket, but the tackle shop was shut. And here comes the bailiff. Which one will it be? Nice Norman, who will only give you a mild ticking-off and sell you a ticket on the spot?

21

Or Raging Bull Reggie, who will confiscate your tackle, stamp on your basket and knot your swingtip? Remember you have only two courses of action: grovel or run.

Habeas corpuses. You're at the weigh-in with a couple of pounds of dead roach up your right sleeve. Can you slip them into the scale basket without the stewards spotting you? If you are spotted, how will you deal with it – bluff, run or faint?

*   *   *

For the last two games I am indebted to Jan Munro, a lady person from Luton, who wrote to tell me some of her Cause-and-Effect experiences on the bank.

If these two take off, Jan, I'll make sure you get the royalties. They don't call me Honest John for nothing. (They have to be heavily bribed to do it.)

Wild and woolly wopsies. On an otherwise crowded stretch of bank there are three empty pitches. If you're not to be too late, you have to rush over to one, slam your basket down and sit on it. Small snag: under one of the three pitches is a large wasps' nest. Will you be the one to get the hot seat?

Even wilder wibbly wobblies. You are sitting close to your deadly match rival in the last ten seconds before the whistle. Each has a tremor on his float. Between the two of you squeezes a lovely lady person wearing a shocking pink bootlace bikini. First one to take his eyes off the float is a sissy.

No. I've got that wrong, haven't I . . . ?

7

Point of No Return

Halfway through the coarse fishing close season is the
crucial time. The one that sorts the men out from the boys.
The Point of No Return.

You've done all the fiddling about and cleaning up of
tackle you can do. You've run out of topical stories of your
fishing prowess to tell in the boozer. Your wormarium is in
full production and there's no more you can do to help,
except keep chucking on the tea leaves, shredded news-
paper and old socks.

This is traditionally the time for outbreaks of husband-
battering by wives who can't stand a man about the house
all day, getting in their way, under their feet. And after all
the promises they made to love, honour and obey.

Once a year, we're stuck with it. How can you preserve
your peace of mind and soundness of body until the
Glorious 16th of June? Trout fishing is the obvious answer.
But if you're not kitted out, can't get to a trout water, are
stony broke or just don't fancy it, you're stuck with long
weekends of excruciating inactivity.

Uncle Clifford's Worry Corner is in receipt of a survey on
the effects on home life when a man retires early, which
amounts to about the same thing as the close season. 'Some
wives,' says the survey, 'find their husbands' continual
presence at home irksome.' (Some wives, I'd have them
know, find their husbands' continual absence from home
irksome. There's no pleasing some people. However.)

'Some husbands,' it continues, 'learn how to get out of the
way by going to the garage or the garden shed.' Not exactly
the revelation of the century. But you can't spend three

23

months in the shed, dammit. And the little women always want to know why, if you've been in there doing something useful, you always emerge falling about and smelling of the Demon Drink.

Most wives, however, tend to be satisfied 'because of increased time together and help with the housework'. Eek! That's the bit you've got to watch. Three months washing the pots and papering the ceiling is nobody's idea of fun.

The survey offers a civilised way of tackling the problem by arranging 'days out of the house, freedom for shopping, and entertaining friends'. That's the answer, lads. Give the Light of Your Life a treat by taking her down to the canal. Let her share in the memories of your moments of glory in the season past:

'There you are, love. Just down there under those overhanging dock leaves, to the right of that old bicycle frame, that's where I got the gudgeon that qualified me for the Cack-Hander of the Year award. You remember, the fish with only one eye and a bad attack of black spot. And over here was where I fell in after the club social – see that bit of crumbling bank? Could have happened to anybody.'

By this time your beloved should be heading off at full speed for the shops, but at least you tried.

Entertaining friends, that's the next bit. While she's out shopping, give your mates a buzz and ask them to call round at your place for an hour or so of reminiscence and nostalgia. Dress informal, but don't forget to bring a bottle. Such occasions can be really delightful, but they are often spoiled by the reaction of your lady wife upon her return.

So Fred *is* unconscious, but it's only because the excitement of the occasion proved too much for him. Added to which he always gets like that when he's had a few.

The cat? What's the matter with the cat? Oh, it's gone potty? Yes, it happened to walk in just as Arfer was bursting into his rendition of *The Road to Mandalay,* and you know what he sounds like in a confined space. Mind you, it doesn't take much to send that cat off its trolley. Never was the full shilling.

The keep nets on the settee? They're Albert's, he brought them round to mend the holes. There's mud all over the Dralon? And the settee's smelling like an old fish dock? You know Albert, love, he never was one for washing out his nets at the back end, but his heart's in the right place.

The kitchen *is* in a bit of a mess, but that's only because Sid brought round the pike he's been trying to stuff for two months. Brought it round for the benefit of collective advice and manual dexterity; does pong a bit, admittedly.

The oven? Yes, it *is* a bit black, but it was an attempt to economise on next season's groundbait by stockpiling dried breadcrumbs. We stuck a few crusts in the oven to dry and forgot about them, that's all; the black will soon come off with some of that special oven cleaner stuff.

Frogs? In the sink? Oh, *those* frogs... Yes, well, old Mitch brought them round for the garden pond. They're an endangered species, and we've got to do our bit to preserve them. Watch where you're stepping, love, some of them seem to – Oops! Now look what you've done! That's one frog less for posterity, that is.

Tell 'em what? Aw, Pet, they're just beginning to enjoy themselves. But... Ah... Well... No...

Sorry, lads. Time to pack up. On yer bikes...

* * *

So much for the days out and entertaining friends. All that's left is the household chores. At least that's what I thought until I bumped into Mad Mac in the pub.

'What have you got to laff about?' I asked, irritated by the idiot smile which no coarse angler has the right to wear at this arid and desolate time of the year.

'Just been doing a few jobs around the house,' he chortled.

'What's so funny about that?'

'Made a mess of 'em, didn't I, ol' buddy? Total disaster. I was just about to start on the Big One – papering the front room – when the missis stopped me. Said she'd rather do it herself, and why didn't I take myself off down to the pub? Of course, I refused.'

'Refused? How come...?'

'Broke, wasn't I? To the wide. Stony. Boracic. Told her I couldn't possibly go down to the pub without any money.'

'So then what happened?'

'She paid me. Subbed me for a fiver, just to get out of the way before I did any more damage.'

25

That lad's not half as daft as he cracks on to be. From now on you can keep your surveys. Where's that wallpaper...?

8

Dressed to Distress

Dearly Beloved and I had the annual discussion about *haute couture* at the start of the season.

'That fishing jacket of yours,' she said, 'has got to go. Frightened the life out of me again during the close season. Apart from keeping coming into the front room to watch *Coronation Street,* it had the cat on the landing three times.'

'Just its funny little ways,' I said. 'It gets bored in that cupboard under the stairs.'

'Those trousers,' she went on. 'You're going to get locked up one of these days, walking around like that. I could never hold my head up in Tescos again.'

'Very healthy, all that ventilation,' I said. 'It's a proven medical fact.'

'And those socks,' she went further on. 'I'd have put them in the incinerator myself if I wasn't afraid they'd bite me. Now you just get yourself kitted out properly. And this time, get something that looks smart. Every year you get an invitation to the Tramps' Ball at the *Boot and Slipper.* And every year there's a P.S. saying, "Come just as you are".'

I put up my usual spirited defence, i.e. went to the boozer and sulked for a couple of hours, before going back home and, very firmly, capitulating. Well, she did have a point. It gets embarrassing when old ladies get palpitations at the sight of you, and stray dogs take a chunk out of your leg.

Being not quite *au fait* with current fashion trends, I invested in a posh publication which had a fashion feature on what the well-dressed fisherman is wearing this year.

The lady fashion writer was going all breathless about rough clothes and tough clothes, which are not only *the* thing at the moment, but which match the rugged appearance and lifestyle of the angler. There were pictures of a male model playing a typical rugged angler wearing the things. He looked rugged enough, I suppose, but he was hardly a typical angler. Too good looking for a start, a full set of teeth and both his ears.

The old-clothes look, it seems, is in. All the gear is pre-crumpled and pre-faded – *distressed* was the word used to describe the look – and was not supposed to be ironed or anything daft like that.

'That'll do for me,' I thought, and turned to the list of prices to see how much I'd have to pay for looking distressed.

Eek!

Indigo blue rough weave overshirt £59.95. Fifty nine pounds ninety five pee? Obviously a misprint. Shame, in such a prestigious publication.

But no. *Cream collared T-shirt £21.* Not that any real angler would wear a cream collared T-shirt, but if he did he could get one for a fiver with the brewery's name on it. *Ink blue baggies £43.* The baggies were presumably the trousers. Forty three quid? For a pair of baggy pants?

Gritting both my teeth, I read on. *Belted blouson* (whatever that is) *£79. Baggy linen trousers with top-stitch detail £89. Summer weight parka with multi pockets, drawstrings and hood £110...*

Enough! There was a lot more where that came from, but I couldn't take it; especially after I'd worked out the prices in pints of draught bitter, which was very distressing indeed. No, I thought. I can look crumpled, faded and highly distressed for nowt. All the old gear was still there, in the cupboard under the stairs. I don't care if I do get locked up. And to hell with Tescos.

Right, then. Let's be having you. The old jacket first. Here, boy! Come to Poppa – Ouch! Down, boy, down! Aaaarrrgh! DOWN! I say...

* * *

Talking about distress... The hot spells of summer resulted in plenty of creepy-crawlies to use as wild bait by those of us

28

given to experimentation: caterpillars, grasshoppers, earwigs, woodlice and the like. And there's been the odd distressing incident caused by the bait's reaction to being hooked. There's been a plague of little hairy caterpillars, for instance – offspring of the brown-tail moth – which cause a very painful rash on humans. It's a bit late for the caterpillar by the time it's got a hook in its wotsits, but at least it makes its annoyance felt, and ensures that the angler leaves its mates alone.

Anglers rendered spotty and screaming by this caterpillar can take comfort in the fact that it could be worse.

There's news from Brazil of a termite that takes even more drastic action: it explodes. If it's prodded in any way or attacked by a predator, such as an ant, it just goes *bang!*, covering the ant with a sticky substance that sets like concrete, and letting loose a smelly chemical that lets other termites know there are ants about. The reaction of other termites is often to go bang as well at the first sniff, so that the nest is surrounded by exploding termites, stiffened ants and a funny smell

British anglers have enough social problems as it is, being thrown out of pubs for ponging, without having to sit there smelling of dead termite, slowly stiffening, and having to say 'Pardon' every time one goes off in the bait tin.

Better the distress you know. I always say...

9

A Funny Old Week

It was one of those funny weeks. Funny unreal, not funny ha-ha.

My difference of opinion with Dearly Beloved about the state of my fishing outfit resulted in my having to wear a new pair of trousers to the canal. Not exactly new, but allegedly in much better nick than the old ones.

As I was walking along the towpath I felt a distinct breeze around the portals. A surreptitious check revealed that the zip had bust. If I'd been wearing my usual fishing jacket, which reaches down to my knees, it wouldn't have been so bad, but on account of the hot weather I was wearing a lightweight bum-freezer which revealed all. So I carried the keepnet in front of me like a king-sized fig leaf whenever any lady persons approached, dropping it after they'd passed because it made my arm ache and gave me a funny walk.

It's surprising how vulnerable you feel with your flies undone. I was passing an overgrown bit of bank when *Whoosh!* - out from the reeds flapped an enormous grey shape with a wicked long beak, straight across my bows. Eek! Back went the keepnet, quick as a flash.

It was a heron. I needn't really have worried, as a heron's diet is mainly fish and frogs, but for all I knew it could have had a thin time of it that morning.

I finally settled down on the bank, back to the audience. No problems. Except - Wassat! A long black flying thing, big as a dragonfly, only it wasn't a dragonfly, doing some low-level aerobatics. After flailing at it with the landing net for a bit, I leapt up and hid further down the bank until it went away in search of some other angler whose defences were down.

It must have been the season for long black flying things (which a detailed perusal of *Creepy Crawlies of the British Isles* has still failed to identify), because a little later one appeared over my left trouser kneecap, crawling determinedly onwards and upwards. This one wasn't a long black flying thing, as it didn't have any wings. But it was definitely a long black crawling thing and undoubtedly related to the long black flying thing, as could be deduced from its size, shape, colour and evil intent.

After I'd stopped screaming and leaping about, I tucked my pants into my socks. No point in beating off the frontal assaults if they could achieve their objective unnoticed by creeping up inside my trouser legs.

Settling back down again, I could still hear screaming. Funny, that. I'd never noticed an echo on the Grand Union before. But it wasn't an echo. It was an original and genuine all-British angler's scream, coming from a bloke along the bank.

Throwing modesty to the winds, I ran up to him in case he needed any advice on what to do about long black flying things, but his was a different problem. He was staring at his float and muttering. 'It's gone. Now people will think I'm barmy...'

'What's gone?' I asked.

'That green thing. With four legs and a snaky head. And a shell on...'

Dear me. Must go. Got enough problems as it is, without loonies who see four-legged green snaky things with shells on.

'No, honest,' he said. 'Got tangled up with the line under the float. Some sort of turtly thing it was – terrapin, that's it.'

Suddenly I felt faint. There I'd been sitting just a few yards further up, with flies akimbo, when there were terrapins in the cut. Probably another pet shop gone bust. Not that terrapins could do much harm, but what if the pet shop owner had emptied all his redundant aquatics into the canal? A few snapping turtles, perhaps. And the odd alligator. Bring back the long black flying things.

*   *   *

In the pub later on, unscathed but in need of sedation, and ignoring questions from the landlord about why I had to carry the keepnet in front of me when I went to the bar, I bumped into Young McGinty Number One, just back from his honeymoon. (Gad, where *does* the time go?)

'Had a nice honeymoon, then?' I asked.

'Smashing,' he said. 'I went fishing *five* times. Got stuck into this beautiful carp...'

That's what I like to hear. A lad who's got his priorities right.

I told Young McGinty about the close encounter with the four-legged snaky green thing with a shell on. The lad at the next table overheard, and chimed in: 'Funny, that. I was with a mate of mine fishing a pond in Surrey last week, and he caught a terrapin too. Only his was yellow and green.'

And what did I see in the paper the following week? A report from Liverpool about terrapins in the Leeds-Liverpool canal. Where were they all coming from? And how far had they spread? I rang up cousin Jim in Leeds.

'Have you seen any terrapins in the cut at your end?' I asked.

'Terrapins?' said Jim. 'Now let me see. Terrapins...'

After giving it some thought, Jim said, 'No. No terrapins. Some funny things outside *The Prospect* at chucking-out time, but so far no terrapins.'

That's all right, then. They haven't made it over the Pennines yet. Obviously have no head for heights.

... Neither Young McGinty's piscatorial honeymoon nor rampaging herons really had anything to do with long black flying things, long black crawling things, four-legged green snaky things with shells on, or my zip busting. Just thought I'd mention them, that's all. To show that it was one of those funny weeks.

Funny unreal, not funny ha-ha.

10

I do Like to be Beside the – Aaargh!

By popular request (at least, from the lady loo attendant on Brighton pier who asked me to watch what I was doing with that squid or she'd have the lor on me) a sea-fishing check list from PIFFLE, the Parker Institute for Failsafe Fishing and Long-term Enjoyment.

Fishing from pier and beach seems to result in more accidents than freshwater fishing. Could be because bait and tackle are bigger, perhaps because there are more people about. Or simply that the anglers are on holiday and full of euphoria and draught bitter. Keep this list by you. It might save a trip to the first aid room, or having your name put in the pier-end Naughty Book.

Happening You have stood on the pier all morning with not so much as a nibble. You tie the rod to the rail, clip a bell on the top and walk up to the bar, which is ten minutes away from closing. Just as your hand reaches the door, the bell rings.

Cause Sod's Law. Merely the application of Sod's First Law of Angling. You have a choice:

(a) Dash back immediately and reel in to find you have hooked the Corporation crab or the stern of a passing boat. During this time the bar closes.

(b) With ears switched off and eyes fixed firmly ahead, go into the bar and have a pint. When you return the bloke on the next pitch will have reeled in for you, and be standing for his photograph holding the season's record. (Sod's Second Law of Angling.)

Happening The large man walking along the pier suddenly does a double somersault as he approaches your pitch, picks himself up and walks towards you with a purposeful and murderous look in his eye.

Cause He has slipped on the bits of mackerel you left lying about. You can counter his approach by one of several techniques:

(a) Look him sternly in the eye and tell him to get lost.

(b) Say the bits of mackerel belonged to the bloke who has just left.

(c) Plead high blood pressure, dicky heart or chronic piles.

(d) Apologise profusely and grovel disgustingly.

(e) Faint.

Happening You ignore the sign saying DANGER: NO FISHING FROM THIS JETTY. Ten minutes later you are treading water and hoping the lifeboat hurries up.

Cause The boarding on the jetty really *was* rotten. All the time you thought it was just the pier management being awkward.

Happening You get to the pier-end bar, shout, 'Four pints, please!' and stick only two fingers in the air.

Cause The dead conger you were unhooking wasn't as dead as it looked.

Happening You are standing there, concentrating on the twitch at the rod tip, when you feel a severe pain in the region of the right big toe, and get home with your welly toecap missing.

Cause However dead that conger looked, it certainly wouldn't lie down.

Happening You are using a handline, coiled carefully at your feet, and really give it the Geoff Capes treatment for the longest cast ever. Suddenly you are trussed up from toe to head, wearing a very fetching earring consisting of a 2/0 hook and a piece of long-dead squid.

Cause You had your foot on the line. Again.

Happening You are chatting on the pier to a nubile

maiden, dressed only in a bootlace bikini – the nubile maiden, not you (I hope) – who has stopped to admire your catch. Just as your blood pressure is turning critical, there is a quiet cough behind you.

Cause The wife, who you thought was safely shopping. You feel such a fool being led away by the ear. Especially the one with the 2/0 hook in it.

Happening You catch a skate and pick it up by the tail. Five minutes later you are being carted into the first aid room, screaming bravely.

Cause It wasn't a skate. Thought by now you'd have known a thornback when you saw one.

Happening Your terminal rig snags on the pier supports. Ignoring the notice about climbing down being forbidden on pain of death, you climb down and unhook your rig. Suddenly the top of the pier looks an impossible distance above you, and you have to beg aid and assistance from the bloke in the peaked cap who is already demanding your name for his Pier Attendant's Naughty Book.

Cause You're not as young as you used to be. Silly old duffer. Climbing down is the easy bit. Wait till the wife sees the summons.

Let's leave the dangers of a crowded pier and move out to the wide open spaces of the beach. No harm could come to you here. No...?

Happening You leap from rock to rock, taking extra special care to watch out for patches of slippery seaweed. Suddenly you are decidedly damp and back into the yelling and spluttering routine.

Cause In taking extra special care about slippery seaweed, you forgot about stranded jellyfish.

Happening You find yourself surrounded by a lot of people with no clothes on, staring at you in horror and disbelief. You scruffy, over-dressed thing, you.

Cause You have wandered onto the nudist beach. Be sure to look behind you when you cast. Better still, move on. It'll save all that eyestrain and shaky baiting-up.

Happening You are fishing an incoming tide from the foot of the cliffs and doing very well. There's a strip of dry beach on each side of you, so plenty of time for another cast. Ten minutes later you walk along the strip of beach, past a rocky outcrop, and find the waves knocking hell out of the cliff around the corner. So you turn back and – Eek!

Cause You didn't check on the local tidal eccentricities. Silly Billy. But don't panic. You have three courses of action:

    (a) Swim.
    (b) Climb.
    (c) Scream.

As his mate said about the deceased angler, lying bronzed in his coffin after a seaside accident: 'There's one consolation, lads – at least the fresh air did him good...'

11

Sting in the Tale

Gentle soul though I am, and normally averse to harming any of God's creatures, I have no compunction about wasp bashing. ('Take that, you swine! Die, you little flamer, die!')

It goes back to my National Service days when, standing to attention on a summer parade in shirtsleeve order, I was stung three times by a wasp which had crawled inside my shirt. I didn't dare move, because of the nasty squad corporal who had promised me the inside of the guardroom at the next available opportunity. And I tried hard not to sweat, on account of reading somewhere that wasps don't like it. But did the little devil take any of this into consideration? Did it heck. Three stabs with its stabber, then off into the Wild Blue Yonder with a maniacal laugh.

Mad Mac, too, has a thing about wasps. Even worse than mine, if his jumping out of my moving car when a wasp flew in is anything to go by. Good job he landed on his head or he might have hurt himself.

Big McGinty used to have no fear of wasps at all. But he changed his mind when we tried to get the grubs from a nest at the back of his garage.

We were armed with aerosol cans guaranteed to kill all known wasps. But nobody had told *them*. McGinty and I, closely followed by his daft dog, did a 100-metre sprint fast enough to qualify for the Cowards' Olympics.

Since then I have had a sure fire method for obtaining wasp grubs for bait; let somebody else get 'em. (You can always spot the local wasp grub expert. He's the one who turns up in the pub covered in bumps and bandages, mouth and eyes all swollen up, who asks for either a Gint of Gitter or a Phint of Phitter.)

There's no denying that wasp grubs are marvellous bait. Having failed miserably myself, though, I would not presume to tell anybody else how to collect them. Aerosol death dealers do not seem to deal much death when the adult wasps have got their paddy up. There is some highly poisonous stuff which does work, but its application is not recommended in the hands of anybody but Min. of Ag. experts on account of the number of dead anglers found lying among the dead wasps.

That said, I have come across a couple of tips for locating nests, which I pass on for anybody brave or daft enough to want to try.

The first one is to follow a badger. Badgers are very partial to wasp grubs and their thick coats keep the stings out. There are a couple of snags. Inner city areas, and even suburbs, tend not to hold a large badger population. You could be sitting around for forty years in deepest Manchester waiting for a badger to turn up. Even if one did, it would probably be lost, and badgers with no sense of direction aren't likely to be much good at finding wasps' nests. Apart from their being prone to feeling flat when they try to cross the M62.

Another snag is that badgers don't come out until after dark. You can follow them, though, with a torch shaded red. The dim red light doesn't disturb the badger, but neither does it give enough light to stop you walking into trees or falling down holes. A badger which hears a heavy crash and agonised howls is likely to suspect that something is amiss.

Should you succeed and come upon the badger ripping up the nest, don't try to take it away from him. Badgers have powerful jaws with a locking device. This means that a bite can be released only with the badger's consent or upon the death of the badger. Hungry badgers do not consent easily. And are difficult to bash to death when you've only one hand left to do it with.

Don't know why I mentioned badgers, really.

One surefire method, however, according to a Major person who wrote to *The Times*, is to cover a wasp with flour. A flour-covered wasp, he said, would go 'zooming in a straight line' to its nest.

This was followed by letters from two people who tried it. The first lived in a flat in London. He found a wasp eating a peach in his fruit bowl. Quick as a flash he covered it in flour, took it down to the street, and released it.

When he got back to his flat, there was the flour-covered wasp back in the fruit bowl and having another go at the peach. From this he concluded that the Major person's theory applied only to country wasps. Town wasps are much too bright to fall for a trick like that.

The next correspondent tried it in the country. He caught a wasp in his garden, covered it with flour, and let it go. Sure enough, it zoomed off in a straight line down the garden. He followed at a swift run.

While he was waiting for the bruising to go down, he concluded that wasps were observant little things. Leastways, this one noticed the brick wall at the bottom of the garden. He didn't.

Perhaps the safest and most reliable method of all is to wait until September or October. Nest discipline is beginning to break down at this time, on account of the worker wasps getting smashed out of their tinies on ripe fruit. They're on the booze all day, don't give a damn about the grubs, and are also too happy to sting anybody.

So all you've got to do is to look for a bunch of wasps singing *Dear Old Pals,* give them some ripe fruit to keep them topped up, and nick the nest.

I should be interested to hear from anybody who tries this. On the other hand, forget it. Lawsuits I can do without.

12

Nobody Does it Like Dennis

If there's a wrong way to do it,
A right way to screw it up . . .

I used to think that song was written for me. Nobody does it like Clifford. But I've just had news of my old mate Dennis from his brother Walter. And from now on I'll give Dennis my award for Disaster Area of the Year.

I'd not seen Dennis or Walter, or their two other brothers, for ages. Suddenly at Blackpool, out of the blue – well, out of Uncle Tom's Cabin – appeared Walter.

Hey up, our Walter. Nice to see you. How's Tommy? Fine, fine. How's John? Fine, fine. How's Dennis?

Pause while Walter falls about and laffs immoderately. Obviously, Dennis hadn't changed a bit.

A perfectionist, our Dennis. When he took up fishing, he took it up properly. Even for a trip to the canal he packs more gear than the average Everest expedition; he's got umbrellas, windbreaks, tents, sleeping bags, stoves, and enough rods to equip the National.

And the clothes; tailored fishing jacket, immaculate waterproof trousers, elegant waders, wellies or ammunition boots depending on the occasion and the weather, enough hats to kit out an Easter parade – bush hat, baseball cap, deerstalker and John West sou'wester – all covered in badges, plugs, spinners and flies.

He reads all the books, does our Dennis. All the angling papers and magazines. There's nothing Dennis doesn't know about fishing.

There's just one small snag. Whenever he puts his

theories to the test, with super-duper gear to test it with, things start falling apart.

There was, for instance, The Monster Pike. Dennis was deadbaiting and there hadn't been a lot happening. To be more precise, nowt, which was sad, because our Dennis had always wanted a big pike, and he was doing all the right things in his attempt to get one.

He was casting over the far side of a bed of reeds, which reached right to the near bank, and had been whiling away the time by making little boats: keel of leaf, mast of stem, and another leaf for the sail. Into the water he put them, at a little feeder stream, and they sailed in convoy around to the far side of the reed bed.

Suddenly – Voomph! A great swirl in the water and one of the boats disappeared. A minute later – Voomph! Another boat disappeared. Pike! And a biggie!

What Dennis should have done – in retrospect and with hindsight, which is always the easiest way to do it – was to have fixed some snap tackle on to the next boat. But no, he got out his spinning rod, tied on a surface plug, cast out beyond the reeds and started reeling in.

The plug came to the reeds untouched. Dennis gave it a flip which carried it over the top and – Voomph! Straight after it, out of the water, thrashing over the top of the reeds and heading straight for the bank came a 25-pounder with a mouth like a jugful of nails. Dennis screamed, turned and ran. By the time they got him down from the trees, the pike had flipped back off the reed bed, into the water, and disappeared.

He was ashamed, poor lad, but he needn't have been. The sight of a big pike, leaping clear out of the water and bucketing across the top of a reed bed straight for your vitals is enough to make the bravest and hardest among us rush to join Chickens Anonymous.

*   *   *

Dennis redeemed himself with the Six-Foot Conger. This time it was Walter who chickened out, for the very good reason that the conger was a lot taller than he was.

Dennis was fishing from the top of a harbour wall, when he got into something good. It took him half an hour to get

43

it to the foot of the wall, and he had still not managed to pump it to the surface.

'Get down them steps, our Walter,' he said, 'and grab it when it comes up.'

Walter did as he was bid. At least he got down the steps and waited for the thing to surface. What came up was a conger. A fearsome spectacle, even as congers go. The bits of its mouth not filled with teeth were filled with rusty old hooks and enough wire traces for an Atlantic cable. Three feet of the thing came out of the water before it turned and dived.

'Next time it comes up, our Walter,' shouted Dennis, taking the whole situation in hand from the top of the wall, 'grab it.'

Next time it came up, four feet of it this time, with enough left below the surface to carpet the stairs, Walter was ready with his trusty knife. As it reared out of the water, thrashing and snapping, he lunged. And cut the line neatly, just above the trace.

'What did you do that for?' howled Dennis.

'My name,' said Walter, 'is Cupid. Not Stupid.'

* * *

The Great Mackerel Haul probably hurt Dennis most of all. Walter and Dennis with their two brothers, their wives and kiddiwinks, had chartered a mackerel boat. The others were happy with the broomstick rods and tatty old plastic feathers provided by the skipper, but not Dennis. He was got up for the occasion in his best Papa Hemingway outfit; bush jacket, green eyeshade, rope soled sandals, a superb lightweight rod and a set of the most exquisite lures made from real feathers.

They had not been trolling for more than five minutes when Walter and the other brothers, their wives and kiddiwinks, started hauling in mackerel six at a time. Not Dennis. At the sensitive end of his expensive rod there was nary a pluck.

'What you want to do...' the skipper began.

'I'm perfectly all right, thank you,' said Dennis, dead huffy. 'I've done this before, you know.'

Two hours later the boat turned for home. Up to the gunwales in mackerel, caught by everybody but Dennis.

'I can't understand it,' he sobbed. 'I just can't understand it.'

'What I tried to tell you,' said the skipper, 'was that my gear had heavy leads to pull the feathers down to the shoal. Your lead was too light for the speed of the troll – you were pulling your feathers clear over the top.'

The families headed back to their caravan site with as many mackerel as they could carry between them – still only a quarter of the catch. Before they dished out fish to the whole site, they lined up for a photograph, with Dennis looking the most professional of them all and striking a heroic pose.

'Hey up, our kid,' said Walter. 'Gerroff this picture.'

'Why?' said Dennis.

'Because if there's one thing I can't stand, it's false pretences.'

. . . Within half an hour the smell of cooking mackerel pervaded the whole site. In every caravan, families were sitting down to a delicious meal.

When Dennis's was put in front of him, he said, 'Take it away.'

'Why?' asked his Ever Loving. 'You know you're fond of mackerel.'

'Fond?' said Dennis. 'Fond? I can't *stand* the bloody things!'

*　　*　　*

Finally, there was the episode of The Viking Helmet.

The four brothers were night fishing on a Scottish loch. Dennis had all the gear. If he'd struck into Nessie herself, he'd have been able to handle her on the super-duper pike rod and big-game reel.

As he was reeling in, he felt a sluggish but definite resistance.

'Something here,' he muttered. 'Something' – and then leaned back into a copybook strike – 'Gotcha!'

The thing came in with a sullen, slow, twisting motion. The light from Dennis's lamp showed a bowl-shaped object with a hole in the bottom.

Walter grabbed the trace and lifted the thing ashore.

'What is it?' shouted Dennis.

'I think you've touched lucky here, our kid,' said Walter.

45

'Could be a Viking helmet. Possibly worth a bob or two. Look – there's a jagged bit sticking out of one side: that could be the remains of one of the horns. And I bet that hole was where the Viking was clobbered.'

For the next hour, Dennis forgot about the fishing. He scraped off the mud and weed from the object, washed it thoroughly and towelled it dry. From his mass of kit he took a tin of Brasso and set to polishing like a maniac.

Finally it was ready for inspection. The brothers crowded round as he held it under the lamp. It was not a Viking helmet. It was a far-from-mint specimen of an early 20th century enamel potty, holed and pitted, and with half the handle gone.

'Where,' asked Dennis, 'is our Walter?'

Walter had melted into the darkness. As he had mentioned before, his name was Cupid. Not Stupid.

13

Never too Quiet

There are plenty of moans during every hot summer about the effect on fishing caused by the weather. The lads complain of too many quiet patches.

Funny that. Apart from the lack of bites, I don't recall any quiet patches. Though the fish may not be over-helpful at times, every lull seems to be filled with incident.

I am getting cowardly in my old age, so I didn't hang about when half a dozen frisky bullocks came galloping towards me on the bank. Fully laden, and from a standing start, I broke all personal records for uphill cross-country sprinting and stile-leaping. I collapsed on the other side of the stile, gasping and wheezing, while the bullocks cavorted about on the other side, making threatening snorty sounds.

I was prodded in the ribs by a knobbly old walking stick, wielded by a knobbly old farmer.

'You upsettin' my cattle?' he demanded.

Good job the farmer wasn't around the following week when Big McGinty took on the same bunch of bullocks.

Picking up his shirt – he was fishing topless at the time; not a pretty sight – he engaged them with some bull-fighting passes. Not top class *corrida* standard, in spite of McGinty's cries of 'Toro!' 'Arriba!' and such like, but still not bad.

The bullocks didn't stick around for long. Either the bullfighting bit aroused painful ancestral memories, or the sight of a 19-stone half-naked loony going berserk was just too much.

Another time I didn't hang about was when Mad Mac poked a stick into a tree to release his terminal rig, straight into a mass of swarming bees. Mac didn't hang about either, come to think of it. We ran in opposite directions along the bank, each hoping that the bees would follow the other. I admit it with some shame, but I was quite relieved when they followed Mac.

Mac and McGinty have accused me several times of being a jinx. As have others, such as Doc Thumper, Tactful Tetters and Cousin Jim from Leeds.

Why, they ask, is life much quieter when I'm not around?

Nothing to do with me. Sheer coincidence, that's all. It's better than being bored anyway. And the evidence of Press reports over the past few years indicates that bored anglers tend to get into trouble. Anglers with nothing better to do have been involved in any number of instances of cattle chasing, sheep chasing and even pig chasing. And over-indulgence in the Demon Drink, brought about by inactivity, has led to eccentric behaviour on the bank, epidemics of falling in the water, ejections from pubs and conduct unbecoming at match weigh-ins.

One angler even claimed in court that boredom was the reason he had turned to burglary. Admittedly it was the close season, but it just shows how boredom can get you.

It helps, therefore, to find something else to do when the fish are not biting. Something legal. Tactful Tetters, for instance, took up conjuring, wandering around at quiet moments and practising his tricks on other anglers. He went up to one old lad and said, 'Would you be surprised if I took a rabbit out of your pocket?'

'I would that,' said the old boy. 'I keep my ferret in there.'

Mad Mac practises his harmonica. Another bloke I know takes his trombone down to the bank for a blast or two during quiet moments. This has brought him many requests from his fellow anglers – mostly to shut up and clear off – but it's worth thinking about.

John Steinbeck, in his book *Sweet Thursday* describes how a Mexican lad used to take his trumpet down to the beach at Monterey to practise. He upset a lot of people one night, though, by giving a spirited rendition of *Stormy Weather* down the open end of a sewage pipe. Several old lady persons in the town, who were engaged in their ablutions at the time, blamed it on all that Spanish food.

Should you ever be tempted to play your trumpet down a sewage pipe, then, make sure it's something less rowdy than *Stormy Weather*. (*Basin Street Blues*, perhaps?)

Yes, you'll have to make sure that your alternative activities don't upset people. Which is why I hesitate to mention the livening up of the winter sports scene by the Dangerous Sports Club (British, naturally). These intrepid nutcases went down the 500-metre Black Slalom course at St Moritz on a variety of unconventional ski-mounted equipment. It included a supermarket trolley, a deckchair, a kitchen chair (which finished fastest), a grand piano and a lifesize inflatable doll reclining on a sofa.

Perhaps we'd better forget that one.

There's an idea for livening up TV coverage of fishing matches which could be adopted, though. Basketball fans in the States were glued to their sets when a novice technician, who was viewing some naughty cable TV films in the studio, accidentally mixed up the signals. Every so often the basketball would fade out and be replaced by goings-on in mixed company you'd never believe.

Perhaps we'd better forget that one, too, in case it catches on. If that kind of thing happened on the bank, we'd certainly never be bored, but we'd never get near the place. And catch the wife letting you go to another club social.

14

A Long Smelt Want

A right old stir a funny little fish caused when it turned up in the Trent. Match secretaries stampeding all over the place and jumping off twelve-storey buildings with cries of, 'Zander! Breeding like flies! Aaaaaaaaaagh!'

And all the time it was only a baby smelt, separated from its mummy, confused by the thunder of wellies from the bank, and trying to find its way back home. It finished up filling a long smelt want in the offices of the Severn/Trent Water Authority, probably even more pickled than most of the anglers who rushed from the river to blot the zander invasion from their minds. One more martyr to Mistaken Identity.

I'm glad I'm not a smelt, otherwise I'd be certain to finish up in a jar full of formalin. People are always mistaking me for somebody else, and sometimes it can be embarrassing.

Feller came up to me on the canal.

'You're not Ivan Marks, by any chance?' he asked.

'No.'

'Didn't think so,' he said. 'Not the way you've been fishing.'

Cheek. I'd have him know I've been mistaken for some very famous people in my time.

I was on a reservoir once, when along came the bailiff. I was fumbling for my money, and coughing in the embarrassed way you do when you've been caught at it, when the bailiff stayed my hand.

'No need to show me your card, sir.'

Sir?

'No, indeed, sir. Just you carry on and try to repeat last

week's performance. I won't be able to stay and watch, unfortunately, but I'll be keeping an eye on you now and again through my binoculars. By gum, you fished beautifully last week. It was a pleasure to watch such an artist at work. They've never stopped talking about it at the club.'

Off he went, shaking his head in admiration. Leaving me wondering what I did last week. Whatever it was, I didn't do it there. But somewhere, wandering this sceptr'd isle, is an angler of such breathtakingly good looks and superlative fishing skill that I was mistaken for him. Congratulations, whoever you are.

Once in a pub a giant Irishman mistook me for Peter O'Toole. (Mad Mac's doing, but that is another and very long story.) It was all very flattering until the Irishman announced that he hated O'Toole's guts and was about to beat the living daylights out of him.

'My goodness,' I said. 'Is that the time . . . ?'

*　　*　　*

The strange outfits anglers wear often cause them to be mistaken for something more sinister. A Hull sea angler who dashed off in his car for the beach, all togged up for the match to save time, sped past an old lady driver.

She was terrified at the sight of him wearing a 'Ripper' style balaclava helmet and a miner's lamp. She stopped at the nearest phone box – and at the next road junction he was flagged down by the police and asked some very personal questions.

After some fast talking he was released, made the match in time and came third.

Mad Mac also suffers from identity problems. For reasons best known to his tailor (Quasimodo Gents' Bespoke Outfitters), his dentist (Doc Holliday) and his barber (Sweeney Todd), Mac manages to look like every local villain who ever pulled a job.

This makes each trip out with him fraught with the possibility of being picked up by the first passing squad car.

We'd once had a really good morning's gudgeon bashing on the Grand Union and we were sitting in a cosy public bar, telling lies. (After a morning on the Grand Union, what else can you tell?) There was a heavy tread of feet across the saloon bar on the other side of the partition.

'Morning, landlord,' said a cement-mixer voice. 'Stolen car job. I'm looking for two villains. Labouring types. Ill clad. Unshaven. Roughly spoken. Shifty looking.'

'They're in there, constable,' said the landlord.

The heavy footsteps left the saloon bar and crunched round to the door of the public.

'This,' I said to Mac as the door opened and the light was blocked by King Kong's brother in a peaked cap, 'is another fine mess you've got me into.'

* * *

Perhaps the worst identity problem of all is not being recognised when you're supposed to be recognised. When you're the star of the show, and people are asking, 'Who's that then?'

I was giving one of my justly renowned speeches at an angling club. (Justly renowned. Word gets around, you know. I may not be wise or witty, but I *am* cheap.) Dearly Beloved had come with me so that she could kick me in the kneecap if I overstepped the mark.

I went up to the deaf old twit on the door and gave him the tickets.

'You can't come in here,' he said.

'I can,' I said. 'There's me ticket. And one for the wife. With lucky numbers for the draw.'

'You can't come in here,' he said. 'You're improperly dressed.'

'I'm not,' I said. 'I've got me suit on. And me clean vest.'

'It says here,' he said, 'club ties. And you're not wearing a club tie.'

'No,' I said. 'I'm not in the club. I've lapsed.'

'What about the wife?' he said.

'She's not in the club either,' I said. 'As far as I know.'

'Has she lapsed?'

'I've just told you,' I said. 'Not as far as I know.'

'I don't care,' he said. 'You can't come in. Stand over there and wait till somebody passes out.'

'Look,' I said. 'I've got to get in. I'm th'artist.'

'Speak English,' he said. 'What do you mean, th'artist?'

'What I meant was,' I said, 'I'm doing a speech here.'

'That's different,' he said. 'What's your name?'

'Cliff Parker.'

'Dick Walker?'

'Cliff Parker.'

'Margaret Thatcher?'

'CLIFF PARKER!'

'Oh, that's all right then. Better than that other idiot they were going to get to speak here tonight.'

'Who was that?'

'Cliff Parker.'

... The bulge in my jacket is a large stone. So in future, at moments like that, I can crawl under it.

15

Hooptedoodle

I like that word. Hooptedoodle.

It was used by John Steinbeck in his book *Sweet Thursday* to describe things which were interesting enough to be recorded, but which didn't fit in to the themes of specific chapters.

Odds and Sods, some people might call it. But I prefer Hooptedoodle.

Hooptedoodle One

There was this horse which sneaked up behind Mad Mac and me on the bank and scoffed Mac's pork pie. The act established two things about the horse: firstly, it wasn't vegetarian, and secondly, it wasn't Jewish.

Young McGinty Number One went fishing at the same spot, encountered the same horse and established two other things: firstly it's an alcoholic, and secondly, it's not very nice to know.

Young McGinty and his mates were sitting there when the horse appeared and attacked their beer cans. It bit the cans in two and slurped down the contents. When they protested, it reared up on its hind legs and came flailing at them with its front hooves. They got very wet on account of leaping into the water to escape. Then the horse stamped all over their gear, smashing the rods and baskets and leaving the bank crawling with maggies from the crushed bait tins.

The lads were wondering how to get out of all this, especially out of the water, when a little girl of seven or eight appeared with a bridle.

'Come here at once, you naughty horse,' she said. She

54

slipped the bridle over the brute's head and led it away, quiet as a lamb, leaving behind four blushing, thirsty, and very damp lads.

Hooptedoodle Two
Someone who wishes to remain anonymous, so let's call him Bruce Anonymous, was fishing the lake of a stately home when from out of the undergrowth appeared a magnificent cock pheasant.

Being partial to pheasant, and a bit lacking in sporting ethics, Bruce laid the poor thing low with a sideswipe of the landing net and stuck it in the poacher's pocket of his jacket.

Along came the lord and master of the stately home, carrying a shotgun, on his morning rounds.

'Ah, morning, Anonymous,' he said. 'Anything doing?'
'Not so far,' said Bruce. 'But...'

Down in his pocket, something stirred. There was a twitching and a faint noise of 'Buk-buk! Buk-buk!' (Or whatever noises cock pheasants make when they're coming round.)

Bruce broke into a sudden coughing fit and, under cover of it, clouted his pocket. The pocket went still and quiet again.

'Sorry about that,' he said. 'Smoking too much. No, nothing doing here, but I thought I heard a chap round the corner reeling in something.'

'Chap round the corner?' said Milord. 'Nobody else supposed to be here. I'd better check on the blighter.'

When Milord had gone, Bruce took out the unconscious cock pheasant and lobbed it as far as he could into the undergrowth. After a few minutes, back came Milord.

'Nobody there,' he said. 'Beastly chap must have done a bunk. Well, good day to you. And good luck.'

Milord wandered off. A few seconds later there was the blast of a 12-bore and back he came. Holding a shattered, very dead, cock pheasant.

'Remarkable thing,' he said to Bruce. 'I'd just got round the corner when this chappie came staggering across the path. I thought if I put him up I might lose him over the water, so I did the dastardly thing and let him have it on the ground. I hope he's eatable, though. Looked decidedly groggy to me.'

'Really?' said Bruce. 'Well there's a funny thing...'

Hooptedoodle Three
This very friendly but very isolated fishing pub had suffered several break-ins, so the landlord bought a highly trained, completely neurotic Alsatian as a guard dog. In came this mate of mine with a twelve-bream thirst.

'Anybody home?' he called.

'That you, Geoff?' shouted the landlord from the cellar. 'I'm just changing a barrel, but the IPA's all right. Go round and help yourself.'

Geoff lifted the flap and went behind the bar. The landlord heard the screams, rushed up from the cellar and found Geoff on his back with the Alsatian savaging his arm to the tune of 13 stitches.

'Off boy!' he shouted, and the dog let go.

'Awfully sorry, Geoff,' he said as he helped the poor lad to his feet. 'I'd forgotten about him. The trick is, you see, to be introduced first. Anyway, now he knows you, you'll be all right next time...'

Hooptedoodle Four
I mention this one just in case anyone has a frog problem.

Lee Mellon, the hero of Richard Brautigan's book *A Confederate General from Big Sur* (American, would you believe) lived in a shack next to a pond.

The pond was full of frogs, which every night made a hell of a racket and drove him potty. He tried every way of getting rid of them, from throwing bricks to using dynamite, but the frogs always returned to start up again.

Eventually he found he could quieten them for a time by shouting 'Campbell's Condensed Soup!' at the top of his voice. But even that was only a short-term solution and he was going hoarse from shouting 'Campbell's Condensed Soup!' several dozen times a night.

The final remedy was so simple that you wonder why he didn't think of it before. Alligators.

So folks, if you're plagued by frogs and the neighbours object to your bellowing 'Campbell's Condensed Soup!' all night, just get a couple of alligators. Your frog troubles will be over.

I'm not sure what you do about alligators.

*   *   *

Hooptedoodle... Good idea that. Makes a change from animal stories...

16

Carry on Floating

It's worth looking more closely at things floating down the
river. They may not be all they seem.

Naturalist Dieter Plage, filming in Indonesia, noticed a
leaf moving upstream against the current. He netted it to
find it being used by a small fish to protect itself from
predatory birds, swimming upside-down and manoeuvring
the leaf with its ventral fins.

Pretty smart fish, that, smarter than the birds anyway,
who still haven't cottoned on.

A strange floating object nearer home was the artificial
leg which came adrift when a bloke fell out of his dinghy at
Lancing, in Sussex. Luckily another boat was passing, and
the skipper saved the bloke, his boat and his leg. (What do
you say at times like that?: 'Excuse me, is this yours?')

* * *

A ginger-headed object floating down the Lune near
Lancaster was young Laura, daughter of Cousin Jim from
Leeds.

Jim had finally given in to Laura's pestering and taken
her with him when he went fishing from a rowing boat.
Laura quickly lost interest in the fishing and was soon
doing the usual Laura-type things: leaning over the side,
trailing her hands in the water, flicking the odd worm from
the bait tin over the side of the boat.

'Be still, our Laura,' said Jim. 'I'll not tell you again.
You'll be in the water before you know it.'

His attention was distracted when a huge male swan,

which obviously had a thing about anglers, attacked the boat: charging it, bumping it, pecking at the oars, trying to climb in, and finally taking to the air to dive-bomb poor Jim.

The swan gave up when the boat rounded a bend, and Jim gave a sigh of relief.

'By heck, our Laura,' he said. 'That was nasty. Now just you –'

There was a damp-sounding 'plop', and when Jim turned to the bows there was no Laura. Twelve feet astern a little ginger head surfaced and a little frightened voice went, 'Waaah!'

Gallant Jim put down his pipe, took off his specs and bellyflopped to the rescue. He dragged Laura back to the boat and dumped her in, dripping wet and promising to be good for ever and ever, cross her heart and hope to die.

'Just you wait till your mam sees you,' said Jim, turning the boat round and rowing back upstream. 'You won't half cop it.'

Whoosh! went the swan as the boat rounded the bend, returning to the attack with a series of low-level bombing runs.

'I'm getting a bit fed up of this,' said Cousin Jim.

*　　*　　*

My old mate Doc Thumper and his lovely wife Pam moved into their dream house right on the banks of the Thames at Wallingford, in Oxfordshire.

'Just look at that,' said Doc as he showed me round. 'I can look out of the window in the mornings and see my boat bobbing up and down at the bottom of the garden.'

'Magic,' I said. 'How's the boat doing?'

'She's marvellous,' he said. 'Come on, we'll take her out for a trip.'

I have mentioned before that I don't have much luck with Doc's boat. Whenever I step on to it, the boat suddenly isn't there and when I jump from it to the bank, it's suddenly moved back six feet. It's OK for Doc: as Skipper, he gets on first while it's still securely moored. Leaving Unable Seaman Parker to untie the rope and jump for it.

'It's not going to happen this time, though,' I said, as Doc started the engine. 'I'm going to get aboard before you've had a chance to – Yipes!'

As I lifted one foot, the bit of wooden staging I was standing on splintered under the other.

Sperlosh!

'Man overboard!' shouted Doc.

'I know that, you fool – it's me!'

'Yerss . . .' said Doc. 'Lovely place, this, but it needs one or two things doing to it. I keep meaning to fix that staging. Anyway, don't panic. Have you out in a jiffy.'

Exit Parker, gliding gently downstream.

'We get all sorts of funny things floating past here,' mused Doc, picking up the boat hook. 'You'd be surprised. Sorry – did you speak?'

Gurgle gurgle. Gurgle gurgle . . .

17

Any Good Bites Lately?

'It was your own fault,' I said to Mad Mac, who the week before had been bitten by a rat. (It had crept unnoticed into his bag of groundbait and had not taken kindly to being scooped up and squeezed into a ball as a preparatory measure to being thrown in the cut.) 'You should watch what you're doing.'

'It's all right for you,' said Mac. 'But you didn't have a damn great syringe of anti-tetanus jabbed in your bum.'

'I went with you to Casualty,' I said. 'Sat by your side while they dealt with all the drunks and grevous bodily harm cases. Two hours of good supping time I wasted, comforting you until it was your turn.'

'And what did you do when I came out after the injection?' said Mac, still wincing from the memory. 'Just laffed.'

'All I was doing,' I said, 'was trying to take your mind off the pain.'

'Thanks a bunch.'

'Don't mensh,' I said, reaching for the can of John Smith's by the side of my basket. 'That's what friends are – Aaaaarrrrgh!'

A wasp, it was. Having a free slurp on the edge of the can. When my left mitt closed over it, it put the sting in.

'Look at this!' I yelled, waving my stricken appendage under Mac's nose. 'I've been stung! Perhaps I'll die!'

'Tough,' said Mac.

* * *

Mac and I weren't the only casualties around that time. It could have been the long hot summer spell which caused it but, whatever it was, practically everyone we knew seemed to be coming back from the water in a bad way; bitten or stung by something or other.

Tactful Tetters was bitten by a creature or creatures unknown on his left elbow, and it became very swollen and painful. Not a very embarrassing place to be bitten, you might think, but it was for Tetters.

The elbow was the one he always put on the bar. So every time he settled down to tell the story of the one that wouldn't have got away if it hadn't been for his bad elbow, he finished up leaping about and filling the air with oaths and imprecations. (Worse was to come for Tetters, but more of that later.)

* * *

My young Scottish mate, Colin, spent some time beach-fishing in Wales and didn't get bitten once. (It seems that a Glaswegian is an acquired taste.) But his girlfriend did.

She came back from a walk in the sand dunes and announced that she seemed to have cut her foot.

'Away, wumman,' said Colin. 'An' hush yer witterin'. There's a bass oot there Ah'm aboot tae have any minute noo. The noo.'

Colin's lady threw up and fainted. Thinking it was something he said (you know how sensitive Glaswegians are), Colin rushed across to give first aid. When she didn't respond to the first couple of kicks, he resorted to more sophisticated measures and wiped the sand from the wound in her heel.

There, looking like a close-up from a Dracula film, were two nasty looking holes. The poor girl had been bitten by an adder.

Colin felt bad about it later, especially as he'd thrown in a couple of old music hall jokes such as, 'Vy didn't I vipe 'er nose? Because the adder 'ad 'er 'andkerchief.'

Thankfully, the poor girl recovered after a few days in hospital, leaving Colin no more excuses for corny viper jokes. 'She'd adder 'nuf of them, anyway,' he said.

* * *

'What of Tactful Tetters?' I hear you asking. 'What worse could happen to him than his bar-propping elbow being put out of action?'

He was bitten by a goat. Further down the bank, on the same trip, his New Zealand mate Jim MacKenzie, known as Macker, was bitten by a horse.

When Tetters and Macker met up, each disabled from nasty bites in places you don't even like to talk about, they had to support each other to the nearest likely place of aid and comfort, i.e. a pub with a phone. They arrived ashen-faced and staggering, clinging to each other and on the point of collapse.

'Dear lady,' said Tetters, hanging on to the glassy-eyed Macker, 'would you mind if we –'

'You've both had enough already by the looks of you,' said the kindhearted landlady. 'Get out.'

* * *

The last victim I met had been bitten by an Alsatian. The thing loped along the Grand Union towpath and sank its teeth into his leg. Just like that.

'Must have been very painful,' I said.

'It was,' he said. 'For the dog. I don't think it will ever be the same again.'

'How come?'

He whacked his leg with a bank stick. *Clunk!* it went.

'It bit the tin one, didn't it?'

Like it, like it…

18
Off Yer Bike

One of the latter-day threats to life and limb on the canal bank is the BMX bike. For those of you who haven't yet been run down by one, this is a pedal bike specially designed for cross-country racing and stuntwork.

It is ridden by young persons with suicidal tendencies, dressed like Evel Knievel. They wear helmets and crash pads, which they need on account of their tendency to keep crashing into things. What they crash into on the bank is mainly anglers.

The danger lies not so much in the fact that a canal towpath gives them a long straight stretch on which to do their stuntwork, it's that they often arrive on the path at speed after crashing down cuttings with 60-degree slopes. To save themselves going straight into the canal they are obliged to run the bike into some stationary object. This could be a metal bollard or the arm of a lock gate, but both of these lack the shock absorbency possessed by the average fisherman. Furthermore, collision with something hard could severely damage the bike, and those bikes cost a lot of money.

The official response when one of these little loves crashes into you should be to point out that he is cavorting on private property, and if he does not cease forthwith he will be reported to persons in authority. But by the time you've picked yourself up, he's 200 yards down the canal on one wheel and heading for the next collision.

Should one of them finish up in the canal after failing to crash into you, it is incumbent upon you to take the appropriate lifesaving action. Throw him something to help get him safely to the bank, such as a book entitled *The Breast Stroke in Ten Easy Lessons*.

* * *

The towpath is also much used by young persons wearing roller skates, leg warmers and earphones. These are practising their roller-disco dancing, as can be deduced from their gyrations and gormless expressions.

They are not quite so dangerous, except to themselves. They spend a lot of time skating backwards and, because of the headbanging music blasting in their ears, fail to hear the shouted warnings about the next bit of crumbling bank.

It's usually a waste of time trying to warn them, because they assume that any angler who is mouthing things and waving his arms about is getting with the insults, and they respond by making rude gestures in time to the music.

It does give you a chance to use the renowned rapier-like wit, though, as they surface, with cracks like: 'You finally made it, old son – Top of the Plops!' They are seldom amused.

* * *

Another obstacle to a quiet day's canal fishing is the craze for walking on water. This is done with the aid of polystyrene shoes, and the British Waterways Board is quite miffed about their use: not so much because it upsets the fishing, but because the walkers are liable now and again to turn upside down, a position which is very bad for the breathing.

So do not be amazed and awestruck at the sight of some wally walking past your float. Nor must you throw things at him in case he turns upside down and adds to the number who are having difficulty in breathing and making the canal very untidy.

Should you see a pair of polystyrene shoes floating past upside down, you must not just mutter unhelpful comments such as, 'Tough . . .' You must assume that somebody is still in the shoes and take appropriate action, i.e. wait until the next biker crashes into you and throw him to the rescue.

* * *

65

Mad Mac's feet have been a long-standing health hazard along the bank, or anywhere else he chooses to remove his wellies. (Anybody who thinks I'm too hard on the lad should try nightfishing with him and see how long they can stay in the tent with his feet. The current record is 15 seconds, and that was somebody with a streaming cold.)

In the interests of public hygiene and pollution control, I went in search of a cure for Mac's feet, which I offer to anyone else similarly afflicted. Washing the feet in a solution of bicarbonate of soda and water - once a day - helps to keep down the pong quotient. As does a dollop of bicarbonate shaken around the wellies and left in overnight.

It is best to shake out the bicarbonate next morning, if you are not to suffer the embarrassment that Mac did after he fell in. His feet were pong-free, admittedly. But he looked so daft standing there in a pair of fizzing wellies.

19

Mind your Manners

Not a lot of people know that the two most commonly used
phrases in the English language are 'Please' and 'Thank
you'. The British also apologise profusely, saying 'Sorry'
for things that are not even their fault. We really are a
polite lot on the whole.

Of late, however, there seems to have been a falling off in
polite behaviour. Perhaps I'm getting old, or perhaps it's
the fault of the abrasive new Britain, but there does seem to
be a lot more pushing, shoving, bumping and boring
without so much as a grunt by way of apology.

This came home to me last time out when I had a long
trudge from the water to the nearest pub. By the time I got
there I needed desperately to answer a Call of Nature. (You
know how the cold weather gets you.)

Blocking the door to the Gents was a large person with
his back to me, leaning on the Space Invaders machine and
watching his equally large mate press the buttons.

'Excuse me,' I said.

Not a word.

'Er ... Kof kof. Excuse me.'

Not a twitch.

'EXCUSE ME!' I said, as loudly and commandingly as I
could. Not easy when your eyes are watering and your legs
are crossed.

The large, flat head of the big feller swivelled slowly
round, the bolts in his neck creaking menacingly.

'You want summink?' he rumbled.

'Please,' I said. 'I want to get into the Gents. Would you
mind just moving over a bit?'

'And what if I don't move?' he said.

'Then I'm afraid that what should happen in there might happen out 'here,' I said. 'And that's a nice suit you're wearing.'

He moved.

(And I'd lied. It was a dreadful suit.)

It was all so unnecessary, though. And perhaps anglers are the very people to set an example, to prove that the Age of Chivalry is not yet dead.

Take a thing like letting others go first with the simple phrase, 'After you'.

You don't push and shove to be first at the water, for instance. If two of you reach a stile at the same time, step back and say, 'After you'. Not only is this a polite and self-sacrificing gesture, it also allows you to gauge the mood of the bullocks in the field beyond the stile, and to establish whether the enormous solitary beast by the bank is, in fact, a bull.

Should any misfortune befall the poor lad, bullockwise, don't let your manners desert you. Pick up his shattered remains, dust them down and say, 'Sorry about that'.

Should he attempt to wrap a rod rest around your neck by way of retaliation, placate him by doing the noble thing.

'Shame to spoil a good rest like that,' tell him. 'Here – take mine.'

He will be so overcome at your consideration that he will instantly forgive all. Either that or you finish up with two rod rests wrapped around your neck.

When two of you get to the bank simultaneously, don't rush for the first spot. 'After you,' you say politely.

In the true and trusting spirit of angling comradeship he will immediately suspect your motives, politely decline your offer and gallop away to the next swim. Leaving you to settle down at the hotspot while he flails away over the eddying scum of Idiots' Reach.

When you get to the pub with your mate, parched after a hard day's fishing, let's have none of that unseemly rush to the bar.

'After you,' you proffer, gallantly holding open the door. Not only does this prove that the Age of Chivalry is still with us, it also solves the problem of who buys the first round.

Should he be kind enough to take you to your home at the

end of the day, you being a little frayed at the edges, don't let him just prop you up at the front door, ring the bell and run away.

'No, I insist,' you say, providing the power of speech has not deserted you. 'After you, old friend. Meet the wife...'

You can't try that one twice, either.

Next time you get hooked in the ear by your cack-handed neighbour on the bank, don't lose your temper with him. Don't kick him in places vital to his peace of mind.

Instead, calmly cutting off the shank and taking the hook out point-first with one swift tug, put the poor worried bloke at his ease by saying, 'Think nothing of it. Happens all the time. Ha ha. Do excuse me while I faint.'

Try to keep your dignity, even under the most extreme provocation. Should you be summarily dealt with by a large fellow piscator for inadvertantly fishing his pre-baited swim, just remember: *toujours la politesse*.

'I'm so terribly sorry,' tell him. 'Can't apologise enough. And I hope my front teeth didn't make too much of a mess of your knuckles.'

Yes, there's no doubt about it. The soft answer turneth away wrath. Manners makyth man. Do unto others as ye would be done by.

Hey up – here comes Mad Mac, looking skint and thirsty. *He* can bugger off for a start...

20

Charmed, I'm Sure

Intent on some free bait, and having nothing better to do at the time, I thought I'd try a spot of worm charming.

All you do is stick a garden fork or spade into the ground and vibrate it. Up come the worms in their dozens. That's the theory, anyway.

My garden being what it is, I couldn't get a spade more than a couple of inches into the ground, so I settled for a fork, stuck it in the lawn and started to twang it.

I'd been twanging for five minutes or so with no result at all, and felt a bit of a fool because some of the neighbourhood urchins had gathered to gaze in puzzlement at the loony twanging a garden fork.

Big McGinty turned up and he, too, stared pityingly until I explained what I was about.

'No use at all, Colonel,' he said. 'You'll never get any worms playing around like that. You have to imitate the birds.'

'I refuse to start laying eggs at my time of life.'

'No, stamp on the ground, that's what you do. The thrushes and things stamp on the ground with their feet, at the same time cocking their heads to detect the first stirrings of worms disturbed by the vibrations. Watch ...'

So saying, he did a magnificent imitation of a thrush – the first 19-stone thrush in the history of ornithology or the music hall – stamping his foot on the grass and cocking his head to one side.

He got a bit carried away and stamped all over the lawn but finally gave up, exhausted and with not a worm to show for it. His efforts were not entirely wasted, though: I shouldn't have to mow the lawn now for about six months.

'Perhaps the vibrations were the wrong frequency,' I said. 'I know: I'll try a musical saw.'

In the garage was this big old saw, rusted through years of idleness, and it was nice to find a use for it after all this time.

I stuck the end of the saw into the ground and, by waggling the handle, got some very pleasant musical effects. Pity I didn't have a 'cello bow about my person: I could have churned out a beautiful Hawaiian-type rendition of *Sleepy Lagoon*.

Not a worm responded, however, which suggests that the average worm does not care for the musical saw, no matter how beautifully it is played.

The local urchins were by now making signs to each other which indicated that they were not over-impressed by my state of mind. Not that it worried me: every great innovator since the world began was thought to be mad at the time. They thought Columbus was mad; they thought Edison was mad; they thought Logie Baird was mad; they thought – talk of the devil . . .

'Hi there, ol' buddies,' said Mad Mac. 'Enjoying ourselves, are we?'

'Don't you start,' I said. 'This is a serious scientific experiment to charm worms out of the ground.'

'No chance with this ground,' said Mac. 'It's as much as they can do to dig through it. They're not going to come leaping out just because you're twanging that saw.

'What you need is an electric shock machine. A few volts should shift 'em. Hang on: I'll be back in a minute.'

Mac is of a scientific turn of mind, often messing about with black boxes and bits of wire. He returned with just such a box, coils of wire and two metal rods.

'Electrodes, these,' he said. 'I'll just stick them in the ground, give a few turns on this hand generator, and before you know it you'll be knee-deep in worms. No use on this lawn, though. Let's try it in your veg patch.'

He stuck the electrodes at each end of the patch, between two rows of spuds, and turned the handle on the generator. He certainly got results. Daft Cat, who must have sneaked between the spud plants to do a whoopsie, as is her wont, shot out of the patch with a strangled cry and watering eyes.

No worms, though. They're probably still lying underground, fried to a frazzle. And something funny has happened since to the spud plants. They've keeled over.

'Must have turned the handle a bit too hard,' said Mac. 'Sorry about that, ol' buddy.'

As Daft Cat disappeared, Number One Son turned up.

'Hi, dad,' he said. 'Can I borrow the fork?'

'Certainly, me old fruit. What's the matter? After all these years you've developed an all-consuming passion for doing something to the garden?'

'No chance,' he said. 'I just want some worms for tomorrow's bait.'

'And what do you think we've been trying to do all morning? Three of the country's finest angling brains? Where are you proposing to get the worms from?'

'The compost heap,' he said. 'It's crawling with them.'

Dearly Beloved may be right, you know. Sometimes I just don't *think* . . .

21

Jeepers Bleepers

I'm all for making life easy for the angler. (God knows, I need all the help I can get.) But I would respectfully suggest that the electronic lure invented by a biologist at the Severn-Trent Water Authority has gone a bit too far in that it's far too good.

First of all, the lure hypnotises fish with electronic pulses in tune with their brain waves, such as they are. When they get close enough, its power locks their muscles rigid, leaving them paralysed in the water for the angler to net at leisure. Not only that, the lure can be tuned to different wavelengths to attract different kinds of fish: eels home in on three pulses a second, pike on ten and carp on twenty.

The biologist, Dr Philip Hickley, pulled in 169 pike in 2½ hours from a two-mile stretch of water during one of his experiments. And then went on to work out the wavelengths for other fish, including trout.

Dr Hickley sees the main application of the lure in fishery management. But if lures tuned to salmon and trout ever get on the market, there'll be a lot of non-management persons wandering the bank in the dead of night with a warmed-up and unlighted Land Rover parked under the trees.

Is not the lure the answer to every angler's prayer? Dr Hickley thinks not. 'It'll take the fun out of fishing,' he says, 'so I don't believe the ordinary angler will want to use it.'

Such faith in human nature is touching, but can you see the average cack-handed tiddler snatcher passing up the chance to sit in the pub and boast: 'Yerss... Not a bad morning. Shifted 169 pike first thing, then beamed into about 450 bream and finished up with 50-odd carp from the pool. Not a patch on last week, mind you...'

Anybody getting down to the water behind that lad would be on a hiding to nothing. Talk about first up, best dressed. Even if the first angler returned the fish in double-quick time, to have the 'fluence put on them by the next comer, it's doubtful if the fish themselves would think much of the performance:

'I'm getting a bit fed up with this, Arthur. Five times I've been beamed up this morning. Not had a chance to eat a thing.'

'Me too, Sid. Ooh, me 'ead...'

Perhaps Dr Hickley would consider re-directing his research into the brain waves of anglers. Not only could local publicans beam out the message that their establishments were open for quenching the thirsts of the gentry, but they could use the pulses to guide anglers unfamiliar with the area to their very doors.

Or perhaps not. Surveys have shown that the average angler knows immediately when it's opening time, whether he's carrying a watch or not. Something to do with his biological rhythms. And he seldom has trouble locating the nearest boozer: he just follows the pulsing in his nose.

There's also the danger that such a sophisticated system of mind control could be misappropriated by the anglers' Nearest and Dearest to call them back from the bank and home for their tea. What a horrifying prospect: hundreds of zombified anglers packing up and lurching slowly along the bank, arms stretched out in front of them. Walking straight past the pub and chanting: 'I come, my love. I hear... I obey...'

No, it wouldn't do at all. In fact there's a deal of danger in any interruption of the angler's mental functions when he's near the water, as Doc Thumper will confirm.

Doc lives on the Thames, lucky lad, and can fish from the bottom of his garden. When he's on standby, just in case he's wandered along the bank, he carries a bleeper which allows Missis Doc to warn him of any emergency calls.

This worked fine, until one day Doc was having trouble with a chub which had made for a half-sunken tree. He was balanced precariously on the sticky-out end of the trunk, trying to turn the chub's head, when the bleeper went off in his pocket and imparted a severe shock to the system.

What followed was not a comfortable experience, but it did lead Doc to one important discovery: that, unlike Dr Hickley's lures, the common-or-garden bleeper does not work six feet under water.

22

On the Runyon

I am reading again the short stories of Damon Runyon and it is playing hell with my writing style on account of he never uses the past tense. This is sometimes making life very difficult when it comes to writing something in order to make a little extra scratch.

One of the reasons Runyon is affecting me so much is that his stories are set on and around Broadway among guys and dolls whose life styles and occupations are not always strictly on the level, and which are reminding me now and again of happenings on the English angling scene, particularly during contests of piscatorial skill and science.

I am sure that Runyon will love to hear about happenings such as these, and am only sorry that there is difficulty in transmitting the information on account of he is dead and gone these forty years or so, and since then is not taking too much notice of anything except the goings on around and about the Great Speakeasy in the Sky.

He will be interested to hear of the angling contests of skill and science where contestants are helping the odds along a little by the discreet tossing of a carbolic pineapple into the opposition's swim. Pineapple is by way of being Mr Alphonse Capone's favourite word for hand grenade, and though these angling pineapples are not the exploding kind, they are upsetting the fish more than somewhat.

In these contests of skill and science there is also the puzzling appearance of several roach and dace which are found to be dead on arrival at the weigh-in. This premature mortality is perhaps the result of being kept too long in plastic bags up the sleeves of lucky contestants, and croaking it just as they are slid into the keep net.

There is also the worry to the insurance men about the high incidence of accidents and other unfortunate happenings to those honest participants whose skill and science are such that they are never needing to resort to artifices such as a welly full of gudgeon or a spiral lead or two for a quick insertion before the weigh-in. These honest and upright citizens without need of artifice or other aids to success figure highly in accidents and fracas during the two or three days leading up to a match. The accidents are nothing of a serious nature; they are confined mainly to being run down by an automobile belonging to a member of the opposing club, or falling into the canal after six mickey finns generously donated by a member of the opposition or by an interested bookmaker.

I am not suggesting of course that these things happen in any shape or form, but am only saying that I hear of them around and about and here and there.

I think Damon will also be interested to hear about match stewards who bear a strong resemblance to Captain Duhaine and his Pinkerton men. Captain Duhaine and his Pinkerton men are responsible on the race tracks for keeping order and feeling the collars of touts and con men, and there is a certain lack of subtlety about the way they do it. Match stewards are solid and respectable citizens, but are only human and sometimes are taking their responsibilities too seriously. It says a lot for the British way of life that they are not yet issued with peaked caps and jackboots and that no heed is paid to their requests for rubber truncheons.

Sometimes these stewards are feeling the collars of honest and respectable participants in these contests of skill and science who make the mistake of leaving their pegs for a quick pee, or who turn round to say a cheery 'Sod off' to some spotty punk from the opposition who is indulging in a little barracking, brick throwing or other form of distraction. I am thinking that it is a good thing that these stewards are not issued with a Roscoe or any other form of rod, gat or equaliser, otherwise we will be having canal banks littered with dead and dying match-men, some of whom are not deserving of such a fate.

* * *

There is a lot in Runyon's stories about speakeasies such as that of Good Time Charley Bernstein's on West Forty-seventh street, where the bootleg liquor is of such lethal potential that Good Time Charley does not allow his friends or regular customers to drink it. Now I have no experience of bootleg liquor, being too young and law abiding, but it reminds me of the time Mad Mac unwittingly sabotages the prospects of his own team in an angling contest of skill and science.

We are sitting in this pub one evening, discussing the line-up and tactics for the next morning's affray, when Mac says that his home brew is coming along nicely, and that even as we speak it should be at the peak of perfection. Then why, I say to Mac, are we sitting in this pub paying exorbitant prices for something which is obviously the product of a long line of gnats? Why do we not go back to his place and sample a little of this excellent home brew before it passes its peak?

Mac thinks this a splendid idea, and also the justification for a little social gathering of the crack members of the team who tomorrow are to take part in the contest of skill and science.

We call on several pubs around and about, and collect such ace matchguys as Big McGinty, Banjo Fred, Peter the Potter, Little Ron, Mine's-a-Double Dave and such dolls as are undiscriminating enough to be socialising with these citizens or who have nothing better to do than to join us. Mad Mac's Ever Loving is very pleased to see us when we all pile through the door, although she is in her curlers and doing her ironing, and gives Mac a friendly pat with the hot iron by way of greeting.

Now Mac's home brew is very pleasant drinking indeed, and most of the guys and dolls are making the mistake of guzzling it down like ordinary beer, instead of treating it with the respect you normally reserve for sweating nitro-glycerine. Mac and I are exceptions to this, on account of previous unfortunate experiences, and Big McGinty is little affected on account of nothing ever affecting him, except perhaps for sweating nitro-glycerine.

So at the close of the evening, which is well into the next day, Mac is looking around and about to tell these ace matchguys that it is time they are going home for their beauty sleep, of which most of them are in dire need, and that it is an early start for the contest of skill and science in the morning, which is to say today. He is very surprised to perceive that only five of the ace matchguys, including himself, are standing, and that all the dolls are reclining with their eyes closed tight like they are slugged with a sockful of damp sand.

The ace matchguys on their feet with Mac are my own dear self, Big McGinty, Peter the Potter and Banjo Fred. Mac is opining that this does not constitute much of a team, when Peter the Potter rolls his eyes, gives at the knees, and crumples in a heap on the carpet.

'Have no fear,' says Banjo Fred. 'I am living only next door to Peter the Potter and I will take him home, tuck him in, and have him up bright and early for the contest of skill and science.'

Banjo drapes one of Peter's arms around his shoulder and lugs him out of Mad Mac's front door, giving us a cheery farewell in a voice that is not quite low enough to avoid disturbing the neighbours. Although Mac does not have too much respect for the creeps that live around and about him, he shuts the front door to stop Banjo Fred waking up the whole neighbourhood.

All is quiet and we are just sampling one more slug of the home brew as a nightcap, when there is an almighty crash and squall from outside. This is seeming unnervingly like a combination of Banjo Fred, Peter the Potter and a set of empty milk bottles. When we open the front door, this is what it turns out to be. Banjo Fred is joining Peter the Potter in a state of bliss and unconsciousness, and both are stretched out on the grass in little shape for anything even approaching a contest of skill and science.

What can we do but drag Banjo Fred and Peter the Potter indoors, to join the other living dead scattered around and about the house, there to lie until woken up by Mac's Ever Loving, an occasion we do not witness as by that time we are at the canal for the contest of skill and science. There are just the three of us – Mad Mac, Big McGinty and my own dear self – apart from one or two ace matchguys who are lucky enough not to attend last night's shindig.

Our match secretary is in no wise pleased by the non-appearance of two thirds of his team of ace matchguys, and suspects that Mad Mac has something to do with it, as Mac has something to do with most occurrences of death and disaster which happen around and about the club. But by the time Mac has finished with the phonus balonus and not a little of the old ackamarackus, the match secretary is blaming it all onto my own dear self and threatening to do violence upon my person with the sharp end of a rod rest.

He is stopped eventually by the whistle for the start of the contest of skill and science. Mad Mac, Big McGinty and my own dear self are fishing with all our might and main to redeem the honour of the club and get ourselves out of the old shtuckaroo. We have little chance of winning the team weight, on account of our team being only about a third of the size of the opposition, but we are hoping to do far from disgracefully with the individual weights. This is seeming more and more unlikely as the match progresses on account of our reflexes being affected by lack of sleep and possibly by Mac's home brew. Striking fifteen seconds after a float has slid under and come up again is possibly not a technique likely to stand the test of time and appear in a matchfishing manual. Nor is twelve stabs at a gozzer, with eleven of them going deeply into the left forefinger, much of an example to a newcomer wishing to learn the art of lightning fast baiting up.

It is about the middle of the morning when I stand up to stretch a point and my feet get tangled in the strap of my basket, tripping me up and leaving me horizontal, dazed and disinclined to move. Mac and Big McGinty are rising to help me when there is a thunder of feet and my two stalwart comrades are thrust aside by the match secretary of the opposition, who is perhaps suspecting some breach of the rules, though this is unlikely to happen with such a law abiding and slow thinking team as ours.

'Wassamatterwivim?' he barks at Mac, pointing to my prostrate but beautiful body lying across the towpath.

'Gastro-enteritis,' says Mac. 'Or possibly amoebic dysentery, though who is to say it is not cholera or typhoid? There is a lot of it around and about this vicinity. Only last night two thirds of our team are struck down with it, which is why today you may be claiming an easy but totally undeserved victory.'

The opposition match secretary is easing off on the boot with which he is about to give me one in the ribs as an aid to diagnosis, and roaring at our match secretary. Why, he is asking, is his team of perfectly healthy and highly trained ace matchguys permitted to join battle with a team of disease-filled, germ-ridden, highly infectious punks who are not even a team on account of most of them probably being dead by now? He is calling off the match on account of sickness and entering it in the record as No Contest. And before his team and ours are meeting again in any contest of skill and science, he is wanting the whole lot of ours vaccinated, inoculated, fumigated, scraped down, dunked in sheep dip and scrubbed with a yardbrush.

The opposition team pack up and drive off without so much as a handshake, offer of hospitality, or even a 'Get well soon'.

'There's gratitude for you,' says Mac, 'after us getting up from our beds of pain and sickness to be here this morning for the contest of skill and science. I know what you need, ol' buddy – a hair of the germ that bit you. Come back with me and I'll set you up with a couple of pints of home brew.'

. . . Though I dearly love breathing and eating and supping and all the other nice things I am able to do on account of being alive, there are times I honestly wish I am dead. And it is a very strange coincidence that I seem to get these times only when Mad Mac is around and about.

23

Duck – or Grouse

Perhaps it's my age, but Falling in the Water isn't fun any more.

I was stepping back on to Doc Thumper's boat after doing incredible things with a rope and bollard on a Thames lock when the boat moved away and severely overstretched my resources.

'Help!' I screamed bravely as I surfaced. 'Drop me a line!'

'Certainly,' said Doc. 'What's your address?'

'This is no time for old Spike Milligan jokes!'

Once back on board I recovered my composure.

'Gad,' I said. 'That water was taller than me.'

'It's older, that's why, Neddy.'

End of ancient Goon Show routine.

'Pity you didn't read this before you fell in,' said Doc, passing over a scientific-type treatise. 'It would have saved all that screaming and carrying on. Oh, the shame of it. Good job none of the chaps from the boatyard was around.'

'Bugger the chaps from the boatyard,' I said, in my best Eton accent. 'Bunch of bloody wallies. What is it, anyway?'

The message in the treatise was, for anybody in situations of stress such as being suddenly six feet underwater or getting a nasty letter from the bank manager: *think Like a Duck*.

Scientists had noticed that the average duck could stay underwater a lot longer than the average angler, and had conducted some experiments to find out why.

The experiments were quite simple. They tied a brick to a duck's neck, dropped it into a tank of water and noted how long it took for panic or drowning to set in. A bit hard on the ducks, I thought, but the scientists explained that they were really quite happy; though perhaps those who drowned were a teeny bit peeved.

Ducks are used to being trapped in underwater weed. Instead of panicking, they just switch off. All their mental and physical functions slow right down. As a consequence, whatever oxygen they have lasts an incredibly long time. After five, ten, fifteen minutes or more underwater, the ducks were still trying to work things out, looking puzzled but otherwise not too concerned.

In nature, this would give them time to disentangle themselves from the weed, or at least stop them worrying if they couldn't.

'We ought to try this, Doc,' I said. 'Imagine the heart attacks it would prevent if people just went all soppy in moments of stress. It would save you a lot on pills for poorly people, and save me all those whip-rounds in the office when pals have popped off.'

'Exactly,' said Doc. 'Let's just hope it catches on.'

We moored at the next pub upriver so I could have a pint of sedative for my state of shock and botheration. It was a mistake. Whenever Doc and I call in at a riverside pub, one of us is usually in trouble.

Doc, fully paid-up angler though he is, looks every inch an upper-crust boating man. Rope-soled sandals, pressed white ducks (no pun, or if there is, you're welcome to it), shirt with epaulettes, 'kerchief around his neck and a jaunty yachting cap to keep sun, wind and midges off his bald spot.

I look every inch an angler, i.e. a heap. This time I looked even more heapish than usual, on account of being all damp and steamy, and smelling of a ripe mixture of Thames mud, weed and slime.

'Morning,' said the tweedy twit who was propping up the bar. 'Lovely day for a sail, eh?'

'Yes indeed,' said Doc. 'But actually we're going fishing.'

'I should have gathered that from the look of our friend here,' said Tweedy Twit. '*Coarse* fishing, I take it?'

'If he's going to start that,' I hissed in Doc's shell-like, 'I am going to collect my longest rod rest from the boat and stick it right up his...'

'Calm down,' said Doc. 'Take no notice. Think like a duck, remember?'

I tried to think happy, duck-type thoughts as I drank my pint and Tweedy Twit rabbited on about the general dreadfulness of anglers. Throwing things at his boat, using uncouth language and making naughty gestures. Absolute shower. Don't know what the world is coming to. Spot of military discipline would soon sort that lot out. Etc. Etc.

'I think we'd better go after this,' muttered Doc. 'You might be thinking like a duck, but you're looking more like Donald than Daffy. Obviously need more practice.'

Further upstream we found another pub. This time it was Doc's turn to feel uncomfortable. Several enormous blokes in camouflaged anoraks, wellies, bobbly hats and broken noses looked with scorn upon his Cary Grant get-up.

'You the geezer who swamped my keepnet this morning?' asked one of the biggest.

'Hardly, my dear chap,' said Doc. 'I've only just got here.'

'I am *not* your dear chap, John,' said the bloke, shoving his broken nose to within an inch of Doc's (so far) unbroken one.

'Just a minute,' I said. 'I know my mate has got his yachting cap on. But he's one of us.'

'Oh yeah?' said Broken Nose. 'Looks more like one of them. Har har.'

'Sup up, Doc,' I said. 'There's only one thing for it.'

'Quack?'

'Quick.'

That evening, at a neutral (i.e. deserted) pub, we were both able to relax.

'You needn't have worried about the big chap,' said Doc. 'In my student boxing days, as you will recall, I was known as One-Round Thumper.'

'But that was because you only ever lasted one round. Even against the YWCA.'

'So it was. I'd forgotten. A lot to be said for thinking like a duck after all. I've never seen one yet with a broken nose...'

24

The Klyfton Factor

'You're looking well,' said Dearly Beloved as they carried me from the ambulance. 'The fresh air *has* done you good.'

'Aaargh,' I said.

Some miles away another body was being delivered. The shattered remains of buddy mate Malcolm. Whose love life would possibly not be the same for some time, though one does not wish to pry into such matters.

*   *   *

We had gone up to Scotland to deplete the salmon and sea trout population a bit. At least that was the idea. What we ran into was a heavy dose of the Klyfton Factor – the ultimate test of physical and mental endurance, the piscatorial equivalent of Sod's Law – with which I was very familiar, but which took poor Malcolm completely by surprise. And to be fair, we'd gone up at very short notice and at the firm's expense. Trouble shooters we were.

The first mistake was not taking a canful of the Parker pike-strangling lobs. 'No time to mess about,' people down South were saying. 'And it's all spinners up there, anyway.'

So all we took was a rod apiece and some spinners, with Malcolm adding a few flies on account of he's used to that sort of thing. When we checked into the hotel the talk was all about the huge sea trout and salmon which were being taken on *worm*.

The hotel management was not over keen on people digging up the flower bed in the middle of the night, and that may have had something to do with the fact that next day our rooms were suddenly unavailable for an extended stay. I wouldn't have cared, but there weren't any flaming worms there anyway. What kind of a flowerbed was that?

Still, we took heart from the locals' briefing, which was to leave all coarse fish on the bank for the gulls. We wouldn't do it, of course, but it did show the superabundance of fish life around and about. We were shocked but further impressed by the news that grayling were treated as vermin. Deeper into Scotland, brown trout were vermin. Even deeper, sea trout were vermin. And in deepest, darkest, sub-arctic Jockland, there was a very strong distinction made between the silver salmon, which were worth catching, and the 'black' salmon, which were rubbish.

Oh boy, oh boy. Let's get with the rubbish. Pull out a few vermin. But stay – there were warnings of the dangers which could beset us.

Wild mink. One of which, a few days earlier, had taken a chunk out of an angler's welly. Another of which had chased a mouse up an angler's trouser leg. One of these days, predicted the local soothsayer, a mink itself would be up some poor lad's trouser leg and possibly not to his benefit or comfort.

Red deer. Of which there were a lot about. And coming into rut, which meant that the stags were feeling fruity and knocking hell out of other stags, trees and stray anglers.

Still, what were a few mink and randy Bambis to hard men such as me and Malc? Let's get the show on the road.

At the river, we separated. Malc had brought his waders and was going to wander about in midstream. I had only brought my Spanish fell boots, so I would stick to the bank. Spanish fell boots are pretty useless things to wander about Scotland in, being made of high-absorbency blotting paper on account of the rain in Spain falling mainly in the plain.

Another early discovery was that Scottish cowpats are invisible on account of being *underneath* the grass. Scottish cows must be very short or very clever. The pats also keep their consistency very well, presumably on account of all that Scotch mist.

Five minutes away from the car and I was sopping wet, frozen stiff and beginning to smell a bit ripe. So what? Trifling inconveniences compared with the rewards to

come. Once I was over this barbed wire fence and down at the water.

Negotiating the fence led to two more very important discoveries:

1. That the top strand of a Scottish barbed wire fence is two inches higher than the average inside leg.

2. That the ground on the other side is six inches lower than the ground you take off from.

Standing on tiptoe and pushing down the top strand, to compensate for the vital two inches difference, was of no avail when my leading foot hit the deck six inches down on the other side. Though the pain was incredible, and the damage incalculable, I remembered I was English, reacted in the true stoical manner of my race, and screamed through a stiff upper lip.

I am now writing a thesis that Scottish barbed wire was the origin of the Highland Fling, and responsible for the blood-curdling cries of the Highlanders at Culloden. I understand why Toulouse Lautrec only tried fishing in Scotland once. And I now know also what a Scottish angler wears under his kilt. Elastoplast.

... Down to the bank. Cast in upstream and spin very fast down, as briefed by those who know about these things. But who preferred worm anyway, given the choice.

Wassis? Trout... moving fast towards spinner and about to - Aaaargh! Something up my trouser leg! Rushing around and heading for disaster area. Drop rod and clutch afflicted spot. Hope it's not a mink, lusting for human flesh. Haven't any to spare. Not thereabouts.

Crush life out of creature and shake out of trouser bottom. (Sorry, creature, but it was either thee or me.) What is it? Vampire bat? Tarantula? Tasmanian Devil?

Daddy Longlegs. Poor little thing. Still, how was I to know, when it felt like a flaming pterodactyl? Tuck trousers into socks in case of further attempted incursions.

*　　*　　*

Three dozen casts and three lost spinners later, decide to move downstream. Difficult, on account of bank suddenly becoming ravine. Have to make way up through pine woods and climb back down again. Hope no rutting stags in vicinity. Don't want one of those up trouser leg, though faithful socks should keep it at bay for a little while.

Get to clear bit of bank with narrow ledge of stones below. This'll do. Just walk along this fallen log and – Whoosh! Giant thingy coming from under log like stag-sized ferret from a drainpipe. Deafening swishing noise. Coming straight for my – JUMP!!!

Landing splosheroo in cold Scottish-type water. Icy fingers up and down my – eek! Still, better than being skewered on the antlers of a... duck?

Scottish ducks are very big and menacing. Shouldn't be allowed.

All right for Malcolm. Wandering about somewhere in midstream. Perfectly safe from all forms of –

AAAAARRRRRGH!

Blood-curdling scream from along bank. Malcolm. Possibly attacked by scuba-diving stag or blood-lusting duck. Or pulled into the deep by pack of monster mink. Hang on, Malc. Have no fear – Parker's here...

Dash back through pinewoods, heedless of dangers. Eventually find Malcolm, staggering around in shallows with pained expression and funny colour. Just hop over this stand of wire and –

'Don't touch that!' yells Malcolm.

... He'd found out the hard way, poor lad. Wading to the bank to answer a Call of Nature. As a gentleman would. And making long range contact with electrified cattle fence. An experience never to be forgotten. Nor to be remembered, if you don't want your eyes to water at the mere thought of it.

Only one thing for it. Get away from this highly dangerous river and into safety of Scottish-type boozer. Down a few malts to kill the pain and restore the equilibrium.

Into car. Vroom-vroom into Wild Blue Yonder. Which gets wilder and bluer and yonderer. Big place, Scotland. And not a lot of pubs to the square yard.

After hi-speed quarter of an hour, come across lone Jock in tractor. He's probably lost as well, but worth a try.

Excuse me, good Scottish-type person, but is there anywhere hereabouts we could obtain rest and refreshment? And mayhap the use of an intensive care unit?

'Och aye the noo, aboot yer kilt an' Auchtermuchty in the morrrn an' lang may yer pibroch reek wi' a wee dram an' mony a mickle,' he said. Or words to that effect. Which roughly translated meant go back the way you came for five miles, then turn right across the bridge and keep on for another ten and you might touch lucky.

Thank you kindly, good Scottish-type person. Vroom-vroom!

Half an hour later we found it. Little boozer tucked away, east of the sun and west of the moon. So we don't know where we are. So what? Let's get with the – Crump!

Always comes as a shock when you run full tilt into a door which doesn't open. Doesn't do the old hooter much good, either. Nok nok! Hammer hammer!! BANG BANG!!!

Window opens above. Tousled Scottish-type head pokes out.

'We're closed the noo.'

'Couldn't you just open the noo? We're two *bona fide* drunks. Honest.'

'No, the noo. We're open again the nicht. Ye ken. The noo.'

The nicht? A million light years away. The noo.

The tousled Scottish-type head disappeared and the window closed, leaving Malcolm and me to a lingering death in the rain.

They're pretty hard cookies, the Scots, but they don't like to see strong men cry ...

25

Feeling the Pinch

To Uncle Clifford's Worry Corner came a letter from George Wonfor of Romford, Essex, with an idea for easing the pain of poorly anglers.

He was getting a bit restless on account of being confined to the house during bad weather. The doc had told him to rest up a bit and not to take his sciatica near the water.

George put the onset of sciatica down to all those mis-spent seasons lugging hundredweights of tackle and bait – plus, truth be told, crates of ale – along river banks. Either that or all the hours spent sitting upright on his box without a back rest. 'Manufacturers please note,' he says.

Good idea that, a back rest on a tackle box. A lot of gear seems to be made with the notion that all anglers are young, strong and athletic, not to say windproof and waterproof.

Even when you're all those things – as is young James, teenage son of Tony, mate of Cousin Jim from Leeds (still with me?) – a design fault can still do you a nasty.

Last season James bought a big tackle box with a wooden seat. It was a great box for capacity: if he'd wanted to take Bo Derek along to add to his material comforts, there would still have been room. But the width of the strap didn't match the weight when the box was full. By the time he'd got to the water the strap had almost sawn his arm off at the shoulder.

Not only did it not do his casting a lot of good, it caused the shakes to set in as he lifted his first pint after the match, spilling most of it down his jumper.

Being a bright lad, and the price of bitter being what it is, he soon fixed the strap with a collar of foam rubber, but there was worse to come.

As well as being young, strong, athletic, windproof and waterproof, James is a big lad. The top of the seat was made of two pieces of unseasoned wood, which in time felt the strain. Every time James sat down, the two pieces parted. The plastic which covered them eventually split under the repeated application of James's 15 stone.

One day as he stood up, he wasn't quick enough. The two bits of wood closed like a vice on the seat of his pants and James was the star of the match – hopping around the bank with an outsize tackle box clinging like a terrier. He couldn't even turn the other cheek: the box had them both.

'Did you get anything today?' I asked in the pub later, failing to notice his watering eyes and the fact that he hadn't sat down for half an hour.

'Yes,' he winced. 'A row of blood blisters right across my bum. And you can stop that – it's *not* funny...'

No, it wasn't. Cruel of me to laff. At least he had the consolation of knowing that it could have been worse, though he prefers not to think about that.

*   *   *

Back to George's sciatica. Probably the only way to ward off all that Nature can throw at you is to take every protective device you can think of: thermal long johns, foot muff, nose cosy, hand warmer, willy warmer, eiderdown, tent, windbreak, brolly, hot water bottle and primus stove. The one snag with that lot is that you can put your back out just trying to lift it.

I never thought I'd see the day, but I noticed towards the end of last season that some of the lads had taken to wearing leg warmers: those things like footless welly socks that ballet dancers wear for practice prances and which detract during the cold weather from the leg appeal of fashion conscious little darlings.

They might not be a bad idea for George: at the risk of his looking like Nora Batty, they'd certainly keep his legs warm and perhaps help to stave off sciatica of the kneecaps.

The recommended way of wearing them seems to be over

your trousers – otherwise people would never know you'd got 'em – but not, as with one lad I saw, over your wellies. Who got him ready I wouldn't like to guess.

You can also stick a leg warmer on your head if the wind is chilling the old brain and threatening to turn your ears back to front. (It's a little-known fact, except to bald headed anglers who habitually fish into the wind, that a high proportion of body heat is lost through the head.)

Don't expect a perfect fit from a leg warmer used in this way: you'll only get one if you've got a long, pointed head. For maximum warmth you can pull it down to your chin, though it does detract a little from observation of the float and it makes eating cheese butties a bit awkward.

Whatever you do, don't walk about with the leg warmer in this position. You run the risk not only of bumping into trees or falling in the water, but also of failing to find the pub.

There are some things worse even than sciatica.

26

I'll be Doggoned . . .

Funny how things come in threes. It was dogs this time.

I had a letter from Dave Mullinger, of Bury St Edmunds, whose fishing holiday in Ireland was fine except for the number of dogs which chased his car and bit chunks out of his bumpers.

'Are they all like that?' he asked a passing Irish person.

'Oh yes,' replied the Irish person. 'That's why you see so many dogs round here with flat noses. That bulldog over there used to be a whippet.'

Then I bumped into Dave Bogart, hunky American person and ace angler of Upper Black Eddy, on the Delaware. (Follow that, Parker.)

'Ever been fishing with a retriever?' asked Dave, apropos of nowt.

'Nope,' I said. Trying to sound hunky.

'I did once,' said Dave. 'On Upper Black Eddy. [Natch.] I'd got a trout to within five yards of the bank when the dog just lit off, jumped into the water and swam back with the fish.'

'That was handy.'

'No it wasn't. It didn't take long to get the fish off the dog, but have you ever tried getting a dog out of six yards of nylon?'

. . . So there I was, sitting on the bank, musing over these dog-type happenings. When along came a dog and sat down beside me. Nice gentle dog. Just wagged its tail politely and sat there.

Then it started whimpering, dribbling, fell over on its side and began scuffling round in circles on the grass.

Hecky thump, I thought. That dog's not the full shilling. Either that or it's a break dancer.

It was still going round in circles and dribbling when the owner person came up.

'Ah, there he is,' he said. 'I wondered where he'd got to.'

'I don't think he's very well,' I said.

'Soon put that right,' he said. And put the boot in.

It was like clouting the telly when it's on the blink. The dog sort of went 'Doinggg!', sat up, shook its head and trotted off quietly after the bloke. If there's one thing better than the sound of his master's voice, it must be the touch of his master's welly.

It put me in mind of the ancient joke. Something was bound to. Prepare yourselves:

Man on phone to police station: 'Officer, I think I've got a case of rabies here.'

Policeman: 'Bring it round. It'll make a change from Guinness.'

* * *

They don't write 'em like that any more. Thank God. Where was I?

Yes. Dogs. There are 5.5 million dogs in the British Isles. Which makes it almost two to each angler. There must be something about me (probably my socks) because I seem to get more than my share. The average is about 4.5 dogs per trip, reaching a regular summer peak of 10.7 on the Grand Union.

Fond as I am of all God's creatures, I would wish to see dogs barred from the bank. Dogs and fishing just don't mix.

I've lost count of the butties and balls of cheesepaste nicked by wandering tripehounds. And the bags of dry groundbait dampened beyond redemption and with their fish-appeal definitely impaired.

I've lost count, too, of the number of bites I've missed by having a great slobbering tongue stuck in my ear just as the float dipped.

Have you ever had a dog stick its nose in your tin of maggies, take a hearty sniff of ammonia-scented sawdust and then sneeze? Maggies all over the bank, all over the dog, all over you and not a one left in the tin.

I was once pulled off my basket by a thing like an economy-size grizzly. It sank its teeth into my sleeve and was playfully dragging me along the bank when the lady person owner turned up.

'Could you ask this thing to put me down, Missis?' I croaked from my recumbent posture. 'And could I suggest you try feeding it?'

'Nonsense,' she said. 'He's only showing he likes you.'

'What does he do if he hates you? Take your leg off?'

'Come here, Tuppence,' she said. 'Put the man down. You never know where he's been.'

Tuppence! The size of the flaming thing. Thank God she didn't have another one called Fourpence.

So these days, I'm afraid, I am not at all encouraging to Man's Best Friend.

But how do you dissuade them? It's no use just ingoring them in the hope that they'll go away. They're out to play and they're determined that you're not going to miss any of the fun.

It is no use trying to welly a dog. A moving dog is practically impossible to kick, and it thinks either you're playing with it, which it welcomes, or you're attacking it, which it probably welcomes also as the excuse to take a chunk out of you.

All that thundering around your pitch, too, tends to leave your gear in a hell of a mess. Basket, rods, tins, groundbait and butties get smashed, trampled and strewn all over. The line tangles around them all, around you, and often around the dog. Meanwhile, every fish within earshot is heading for the hills.

Inevitably, just as you are raising the old power-packed welly to do the nasty, the dog's owner turns up. There are two kinds of owner: an intimidating matron with a voice like a klaxon and a lethal technique with a brolly, or a seven-foot gentleman with outsize muscles and an inclination to use them.

You could try a touch of animal psychology. Give the dog something to keep it occupied. Teach it to swim, perhaps. And make sure the brick is tied firmly round its neck.

(Only kidding, Dog Lover of Didsbury. Ha ha.)

The best means of dissuasion, I've found, is the landing net handle, applied smartly to the doggie-pog's bonce. It has to be applied immediately the dog appears, before it can beguile you with its soulful eyes, wagging tail and engaging ways. And before the owner appears. This ensures that there is no emotional involvement with the dog. And no physical involvement with the owner.

In the old days, admittedly, the application of a steel or stout ash handle could prove a touch on the fatal side. But landing net handles these days are almost always of a light alloy, and do not really hurt the animal. They bounce off with a reverberating *boi-oi-oi-oinggg* . . . which is quite pleasant to the ear, and which leaves the dog with nothing worse than a syncopating skull.

Still, I suppose nowadays we can count ourselves lucky. Discounting cows and horses, pigs and sheep, and perhaps the odd goat, we've nothing bigger than dogs to worry about on the bank. I've just been reading about the Thames in between Ice Ages, when the banks were swarming with mammoths and woolly rhinoceroses and things.

Imagine it:

'Hey, Missis! Have you got a licence for that mammoth?'
'What's it got to do with you?'
'It's just sat on my mate's umbrella, that's what.'
'Why don't you let your mate speak for himself?'
'He can't. He's under the umbrella . . .'

27

Elementary, My Dear Mac . . .

I had time lately to read the Sherlock Holmes stories again.
What a brain that lad had: able to deduce from a few slight
clues that the bloke who did the dastardly deed was a short,
fat, ginger-haired sagger maker's bottom knocker who took
snuff, spat in the fire and regularly kicked the cat.

With a bit of practice, I reckon I could do almost as well.
Perhaps be able to deduce what Mad Mac's been up to, and
even be able to work out what he's going to do next. Stop
him working so many flankers.

I can picture it now . . .

*   *   *

As the weak midday sun struggled to clear the mists
swirling along the Grand Union Canal, it lit upon the
hawklike and finely chiselled features of Sheerluck Parker.
His penetrating gaze was fixed firmly upon the float which
twitched tantalisingly on the water in front of him. Would
it be a record roach? Or another undernourished gudgeon?
His steel-and-whipcord muscles tensed for the strike which
would soon reveal –

'Hi there, ol' buddy!'

'Curses! Missed!' muttered Parker. And without looking
up he greeted the shambling figure which approached him.
'Mac! For crying out loud! Why don't you do everybody a
favour and lie down in front of a bus?'

'Hey, ol' buddy! How did you know it was me?'

'Elementary, my dear Mac. Who else would come
lurching along the towpath, shouting raucous Geordie

101

greetings at the top of his voice, just as somebody was about to get stuck into a potential record-breaker?'

'Amazing,' said Mac. 'But what a day I've had. Just listen to –'

'No need,' said Parker, running his eyes over the unkempt form in front of him. 'This morning you rose early, packed the cheese-and-pickle butties which your Ever Loving had prepared the night before, and roused her to make your breakfast of beans on toast.

'She was not in the best of moods, having burnt the toast. You were able to eat some of it, however, as is evident from the crumbs on your upper lip, before she tipped the beans over your head after a small domestic altercation.'

'Brilliant, ol' buddy! But how did you –'

'The altercation was occasioned by the arrival of the milkman, a day earlier than his normal collecting day, and the discovery that a five pound note, put aside in a pot in the hallway to pay him, had disappeared. The note had been filched three days before by your own dear self, spent on the Demon Drink, and was intended to be replaced this evening after you had borrowed one from me.'

'Exactly,' said Mac. 'You must be psychic.'

'Not a bit of it. Simple deduction. Earlier this week, if you recall, you surprised everyone by buying a drink, and revealed the source of your unaccustomed wealth. I knew the milkman was a day early because he called also at my humble abode, causing me to dive behind the settee to escape detection. I knew that you would tap me up for a fiver because you do so most times we meet.

'The tipping of the beans is self-evident: there are still a few clinging to your hair and a couple stuck behind your ear. Your unshaven physiognomy bears the remains of cheese-and-pickle butties, which must have been prepared before the fracas, otherwise you wouldn't have got them.'

'Dead right, ol' buddy. But let me tell you –'

'About this morning? You have been fishing into the wind on the unsheltered corner of the reservoir for an hour or two, and have caught one or more bream on maggot after heavy groundbaiting.'

'This gets better. But how –'

'Your eyes are watering, your nose is running and your ears have turned purple: all symptoms of fishing into the wind in the early morning at the notorious spot known to regulars as Pneumonia Corner. And with your customary fastidiousness, you have wiped bream slime, maggot skins and groundbait all down your right sleeve.

'What's more, before arriving at this spot on the canal, you called in at the Three Horseshoes and imbibed three pints of Guinness. You drank them left-handed, leaning on the bar with your right elbow in an attempt to strike a nonchalant pose as you chatted up Miss Maisie Fruit, the barmaid whose outstanding qualities you have long admired.

'On the way out of the Three Horseshoes, after calling in the Gents, you tripped on the step and were run over by a pedal cyclist. At the time, and indeed as we speak, you were wearing purple Y-fronts.'

'My mind is reeling, ol' buddy,' gasped Mac. 'How *do* you do it?'

'Possibly the easiest bit of all,' said Parker, modestly. 'The Three Horseshoes is the only pub for miles which will let you have anything on the slate. And then only when Miss Maisie Fruit is in sole charge. There is Guinness froth in a halo around the toast crumbs. And you have never yet left a pub without drinking at least three pints of anything.

'You were leaning with your right elbow on the bar, which Miss Maisie Fruit always neglects to clean, as can be deduced from the still-damp state of your sleeve. Thus only your left arm was free enough to perform the actions essential for the putting away of three pints of Guinness.

'On the way out of the pub you tripped, because you always do. You are so busy looking at the sign over the door which says, 'Duck or Grouse', that you fail to notice the other one which says, 'Mind the Step'. And the fact that a pedal cyclist ran over you is evident from the tyre marks on the back of your anorak.'

'Fantastic,' said Mac. 'But how did you know I went to the Gents? And how do you know I'm wearing purple Y-fronts?'

'Easiest of all, old son. You've left your flies open.'

28

In a Manner of Speaking

The tackle dealer was well into his sales pitch on the new super-duper electronic reel.

'The tension is automatically adjusted, depending on the speed of the water and how fast the fish is pulling,' he said. 'No chance of a fish smashing you. And down here the reel's got a calibrated scale for your trotting speed. All you have to do is keep your eye on the scale and you can tell at a glance how much line is going out and how fast it's going.'

'What if I want to keep an eye on the water?' I asked.

'No need,' he said. 'This does it all for you. Everything you need to know, right in front of your eyes. At the first hint of any trouble, this little warning device...'

I thanked him kindly and wandered off in search of something simpler. I rather like looking at water and am usually curious enough to want to know where the fish is heading with my rig. If ever I feel an irresistible urge to look at calibrated scales, I can always sit in front of the gas meter.

But the electronic age is with us, and I suppose we'll just have to get used to it. Give it another season or so and the computer lads will have come up with the ultimate: the Talking Reel. No reason why they shouldn't: the BL Maestro computerised car already talks to the driver, giving reminders about seat belts, lights, petrol consumption, speeds and such.

Not only does it do it in English: export versions give instructions in French, German and Italian. Plaid Cymru, the Welsh Nationalist Party, wanted to know why they couldn't have one which spoke Welsh, but BL reckoned the market wouldn't be big enough. Not only that, it could be a hazard to any English-speaking driver. Before he'd worked out what 'Rhowch eici gwregys ar' was all about, he'd have been nicked for not fastening his seat belt.

There was some controversy also about the kind of voice used in the Maestro. It's a soothing woman's voice, quite pleasant to a man's ear. But several lady person potential customers said they'd like a man's voice: one even suggested Dennis Waterman's, presumably with instructions a bit more polite than those he dishes out in *The Sweeney* or *Minder*. ('I said *brake*, fer bleep's sake! Wotcha fink yer playin' at, yer dozy old moo!')

There's little doubt that most male anglers would prefer a woman's voice, providing it was soothing and didn't nag. Few men, unless they were homesick, would want a reel telling them, 'Don't sit there! Not in those trousers! Clean on this morning they were! And don't wipe all that bream slime down your jumper! Took your wife weeks to get the last lot off!'

Other anglers might like a touch of authority in the voice; preferring a real professional fisherman telling them what to do. The most professional of all is the Scottish gillie, but again we could run into personality clashes, not to say language difficulties. It would start happily enough, but the average gillie is not renowned for his patience when the angler does something really stupid.

'Up a wee bit now, sorr. Slacken off when ye hit that fast water. Now gently aroon' yon rock. That's ma clever wee mannie. Now carefu' here... He's gae'in tae lunge intae yon pool an' there's an awfu' big snag at the...

'Och! Ye've lossit him, ye stupit, knockitty-kneed, crossity-ee'd Sassenach eejit!'

Maybe we're best sticking with the woman's voice. Calm, soothing, mayhap even sexy. Possibly the boffins could build something more into the program by way of information and entertainment. Something like the old speak-your-weight-and-fortune machines, perhaps:

'Hello, there. I'm Rita, your personalised playmate all-electronic reel. My miniaturised crystal ball tells me that your name is Sid, you're five foot eight, 13 stone, bald headed and pot bellied. You're wearing the most dashing olive green wellies and a brown pullie with bits of cheese and pickle down the front.

YES — HERE WE GO. YOUR FLOAT HAS DISAPPEARED AND YOU ARE BEING TOWED ALONG THE BANK BY A POTENTIAL RECORD CARP. HER NAME IS LULUBELLE, SHE IS 20 YEARS OLD, WEIGHS 50 lb, HAS HAD 6,000,000 OFFSPRING AND, APART FROM A SPOT OF TAIL ROT, IS IN EXCELLENT HEALTH. SHE HAS BEEN HOOKED 75 TIMES DURING HER LIFE, BUT HAS NOT BEEN LANDED FOR THE PAST FIVE YEARS BECAUSE OF HER GREAT WEIGHT AND ACCUMULATED EXPERIENCE. HER FAVOURITE TECHNIQUE WHEN HOOKED IS TO ...

'The stars tell me it will be your lucky day. Jupiter is in conjunction with Uranus, a sure sign of success.

'Yes – here we go. Your float has disappeared and you are being towed along the bank by a potential record carp. Her name is Lulubelle, she is 20 years old, weighs 50 lb, has had six million offspring and, apart from a spot of tail rot, is in excellent health.

'She has been hooked 75 times during her life, but has not been landed for the past five years because of her great weight and accumulated experience.

'Her favourite technique when hooked is to drag the angler along the bank towards the undercut spur at the corner of the lake, which we are now approaching at an average speed of 5.4 miles per hour.

'Once the angler reaches the spur, his weight usually proves too much for the undercut portion and – Whoops!

'Your name is Sid, you're five foot eight, 13 stone, bald headed and pot bellied. You are also six feet underwater and panicking madly.

'According to the stars, however, this should not have happened. With our computerised predictions we can normally guarantee that nothing can go wrong... Go wrong... Go wrong...'

29

Humpty Dumpty meets Krafty Klifford

You know how it is when you get home a bit late, and your mind is still full of lofty thoughts, and you fall over the milk bottles and the keyhole won't keep still. It was one of *those* nights.

I finally got inside the front door and wiped my feet on the cat.

'Do you *mind*?' came the tinkling tones of Dearly Beloved from upstairs as the cat's howls subsided. 'I'd just nodded off when you started all that racket. And what are you doing to that cat? You'll have the neighbours complaining. Again.'

A fig for the neighbours, I thought. I'll give 'em something to complain about. A little night music. Full blast with the windows open. What shall we have? The Pipes and Drums of the Argylls? The Ride of the Valkyries? Al Jolson's Good Old Good Ones?

I opened the door of my study to load up the record player. (My study. That's the room where Dearly Beloved keeps the ironing board, the washing basket, the vacuum cleaner, the old tins of paint and the deckchairs. Where the kids keep footballs, cricket bats, hockey sticks, tennis rackets and guitars. I have a few books along one wall.)

On went the light and – Aaaaaaaaaargh! On the back of a chair rested two great hairy paws with five-inch claws. And looking over them was a great shaggy head, with big ears, staring eyes, lolling tongue and gigantic fangs. If it's real, I'm dead. If it's not, then the screaming heebies have caught up with me at last. Aaah ... yabbadabbadabba ... help!

'Oh, sorry,' called Dearly Beloved. 'That's the wolf outfit for the school play. I hope it didn't scare you. On the other hand – serves you right. Tee hee.'

Oh, very funny. Highly risible. Tee bloody hee. Could have cut me down in my prime, that could. Into the bathroom for an aspirin to soothe my shattered thingies. What's this? Hanging from the line over the bath – a pair of combinations, trapdoor and all. Another man! Where is he? I'll kill him! Tear him limb from –

'Don't touch those combs,' called Dearly Beloved. 'They're for the school play as well. And so are the sheep's heads on the sideboard. You can try one on if you like – I'd suggest the black one. You being the black sheep. Tee hee.'

Har har. There they were on the sideboard downstairs, six white knitted sheep's heads and one black one. Like balaclava helmets with bobbly bits on top and floppy woolly ears. I did try the black one on. Very fetching.

Over the back of the settee was a very large, loud check clawhammer coat with a label in the lapel saying 'Humpty Dumpty' and a pair of purple silk Cossack trousers.

What kind of a play *is* this? Humpty Dumpty and Bo Peep meet the Wolf Man? On ice?

No matter. Must get my gear ready for tomorrow's assault on the killer sharks of the Grand Union. Where's my faithful old anorak? My lucky trousers? My Man United bobbly hat?

'WHERE'S ME GEAR???!!!'

'Ssssh! I didn't think you'd be needing it this weekend. It's at school. For the scarecrow.'

'For the WHAT?'

'It's only for one scene. You'll have it all back next week.'

'I don't want it back next week! I want it *now*!'

'Well you can't have it. So there. Now stop making a fuss and come to bed.'

Fuss, she says. When all my faithful old clobber has been nicked for a flaming scarecrow. But not to worry. They don't call me Krafty Klifford for nothing.

* * *

... It can be a touch embarrassing, wandering along the

Grand Union towpath wearing a clawhammer coat two sizes too big, a pair of purple silk Cossack trousers tucked in the wellies, and a black balaclava helmet with a bobbly bit on the top and two floppy ears.

But what else was I supposed to do? Fish starkers? In this weather? Getting frostbite in me vitals and arrested to boot?

Tell you what, though. I wasn't half glad to get those combs off. Talk about *itch* . . .

30

On the Sick

They keep having laffs at the Department of Health and Social Security over the howlers on the do-it-yourself sick notes. Conditions which have laid people low include 'flue virus', 'bleeding noise', 'jangles', 'pain in the angle', 'blown-up arm', 'desperation' and a 'fluid stomach'.

One old woman said she was 'sick and tired due to the doctor's tablets'. A Somerset man announced that he was 'mentally unstable' and was 'staying in bed until a psychiatrist comes'.

I hope someone at the DHSS is keeping an eye open for anglers' sick notes. There are bound to be a few ailments so far unknown to medical science: cowpat poisoning, congestion of the gills, lumbago of the lateral line, not to mention outbreaks of basket bum, nightfisher's nose and reservoir ears.

You can see some of the notes already:

'I left my cap off when I went fishing and got chilled to the bone.'

'I put my hand in a conger's mouth to see how many teeth it had. It closed its mouth to see how many fingers I had.'

'Strained myself in pub illustrating the size of the bait.'

'Suffering from short sight. Dropped lucky rabbit's foot in road on way to match. Went back to collect it. Didn't see bus.'

(Not as daft as it sounds, that last one. Mad Mac has always had a fear of being run over and always looks both ways when crossing the road. One day he looked left, right and left again. There was not a car, bus or lorry in sight. So

111

he stepped out into the road and was knocked down by a horse.)

I digress:

'Broken ribs caused by laughing. The 16-stone bloke at the next peg fell into the water during our last match. He didn't laugh. I did.'

'Severely chilled after walking 851 yards along pier. Pier was only 850 yards long.'

'Reason for pneumonia is violent storm which sprang up when I was out fishing. A mate who lived by the river invited me to stay at his place the night. I got soaked going home for my pyjamas.'

'The boat filled with water, so I pulled out the plug.'

'Chill caused by severe waterlogging. Threw out the anchor and forgot to let go.'

'Severe bruising caused by overweight. The rival match team discovered the spiral leads in the fish I weighed in.'

'Broken arm caused by size of mouth. I told 6ft 6in bailiff where to put his rule book.'

* * *

There must still be plenty of questions that need answering when the claimants are called in for interviews:

DHSS Person: 'You said on your form that you had the day off for an appointment with your doctor. Yet you were seen on the river bank, fishing with a little fat man in spectacles.'

Angler: 'That's right. The little fat man in spectacles *is* my doctor.'

DHSS Person: 'You state here that a shark bit your leg off. Which one?'

Angler: 'How should I know? They all look the same to me.'

DHSS Person: 'Your injuries were caused apparently because your wife beat you black and blue after a six-day fishing festival. Why was that?'

Angler: 'She found out I didn't go.'

DHHS Person: 'It says here that after celebrating a match win, you tried to jump the canal. How did that affect your health?'

Angler: 'I tried it in two jumps.'

DHSS Person: 'You say your wife struck you with a flat

iron after you gave her a set of floats for her birthday. Why on earth was that?'

Angler: 'She was expecting a fur coat.'

DHSS Person: 'You say you suffered severe lacerations of the nether regions owing to lapse of memory. Could you elaborate?'

Angler: 'I got up in the morning and jumped straight into the bath. I forgot I'd put a 25 lb pike in there the night before.'

DHSS Person: 'You suffered a severe headache after sitting on a rod rest? How come it was your head that hurt?'

Angler: 'I was fishing under a low bridge.'

DHSS Person: 'You claim severe depression because your wife ran off with your best friend. How exactly does it affect you?'

Angler: 'Now I've got to go fishing without him.'

And there's always one in every club:

DHSS Person: 'You say you are depressed because you can't seem to get on with the fellow members of your angling club. Why do you think you can't get on with them?'

Angler: 'How the hell should I know, you four-eyed, bald-headed old twit!'

31

Ours is an Ice House

You've got to hand it to the Americans: when they do a thing, they do it big. And they like their creature comforts.

Take winter fishing. They don't do it like we do: sitting there all day as fully paid-up masochists, turning blue and seizing up, having to be thawed out when we get home. Watching with dismay as the frostbitten bits go thudding on to the hearthrug. At least in Minnesota they don't.

There's a stretch of lakes there, Mille Lacs, 22 miles long, which freezes over every year. And freezes properly, with three feet of ice.

Every winter there are 3,800 houses on that ice, grouped in 100 villages. Centrally heated, they are, with lighting, running water, fridges, tellys, carpets and all mod cons.

The hardy American anglers are fishing *inside* the houses, through holes bored in the ice. True, there are some hard men who scorn indoor fishing, or who can only get to the lake for the odd day trip. Not for them the molly-coddling of armchairs and central heating. Oh no: they cut holes in the floors of their cars and sit there roughing it.

But for most of the anglers, it's the delights of the Great Indoors. The one snag seems to be that whole families go along and ice neighbourhoods are set up, with elected mayors to make sure everybody's having fun. There are barbecues, volleyball, horseshoe pitching and film shows in case anybody's getting bored.

The whole family. In an ice house 10ft by 24ft. Can you imagine us putting up with it? Telly on full blast when you're trying to concentrate. Kids swarming all over the place. Cats falling down the spare ice holes. Missis vacuuming the carpet just as the rod tip starts to twitch.

And what about mealtimes, when Sod's Law decrees that they're bound to clash with feeding time beneath the ice?

'Yoo-hoo! Tea's ready. Come and get it...'

'Yes, love. Just a minute. Had a touch then.'

'It'll go cold.'

'No, it won't. Stick it under the grill.'

'But mother wants hers now.'

'Well let her get on with it.'

'You know she hates eating on her own.'

'Tough. There it goes again. Any second now and –'

'Sidney! To the table!'

'Blast! Missed it! All your flaming mother's fault! Right. I'll have my tea. And after that I'm taking your mother out to indulge in an old Eskimo custom.'

'She'll enjoy that. You are kind, Sidney. What custom's that, then?'

'What the Eskimos do with their mothers-in-law when the old dears are feeling a bit off-colour. Take them out on the ice.'

'That's nice. The fresh air will do her good. And then what do they do?'

'Leave 'em there.'

* * *

In Britain we seldom have ice thick enough for the ice-house idea to catch on in a big way. Nor even the polar bears to make sure the mother-in-law wouldn't have to spend too long sitting about in the cold. But some form of indoor fishing would have its appeal in winter, especially around Christmas when we are also trying to indulge in a spot of the Ding Dong Merrily.

I put the idea to Arthur, mine host of the *Boot and Slipper*.

'I did hear once,' I said, 'that there are lots of underground streams hereabouts.'

'That's right,' said Arthur.

'And that one of them runs under your cellar.'

'So I've heard.'

'I've got a smashing idea. Great for trade.'

'Go on.'

I went on, ignoring the suspicious look which flitted

across Arthur's classical features, and outlined the plan. Simplicity itself.

Drill a few holes in the cellar floor until they reach the underground stream. The stalwart local anglers could then fish and sup at the same time in complete safety. No chance at all of falling in the water. And if Arthur were to place a barrel at their disposal, there would be no need for service: save a lot on wages. What's more, he wouldn't even have to throw the anglers out: when the pub closed he could just leave them down there to get on with it. Wouldn't be a bit of trouble.

'When you say *local* anglers,' said Arthur, 'presumably you'd include yourself.'

'Naturally.'

'And Mad Mac?'

'Yes.'

'And Big McGinty?'

'Well, yes. Have to take the rough with the smooth. What do you think?'

What Arthur thought was pretty positive. Direct and to the point. The full text was unfortunately not suitable for reproduction, but the gist of it was that he was not entirely in favour of the project.

Pity, that. Means I'll have to face another Christmas exposed to all the hazards of wind and rain, sleet and snow. Force Nine gales in exposed areas and severe frost around the Midlands.

'You do realise,' I said, 'that your heartless decision could well be the death of me?'

'Don't worry,' said Arthur. 'I'll make sure there's a whip-round.'

'No need to bother. I don't want any flowers.'

'I wasn't thinking of flowers.'

'No? What, then?'

'Well, if you include the regulars in the Saloon Bar, I might just raise enough to clear what you've got on the slate.'

Ti-idings of co-omfort and joy
Comfort and joy . . .

32

Kids' Stuff

Any of us suffering from the stress of modern living could
do worse than return to our childhood. So it seems, anyway,
from a scheme for women to re-live their schooldays.

It all happens at a school in Ireland (it had to). The
women dress in gymslips, sit at desks with inkwells, eat
stodgy school food, play leapfrog at playtime and knock
hell out of each other at hockey. And if anybody wants to
bring a teddy bear or have a blub in the dorm, nobody
minds.

The idea could catch on ...

* * *

The scene is the towpath of the Grand Union Canal. Along
it are walking three figures: one fat and lumbering, one
little and whippety, one superbly muscled and with a
stately bearing. None other than Big McGinty, Mad Mac
and Modesty Forbids.

'I say, you fellows,' wheezed Big McGinty. 'Couldn't you
slow down a bit? This tackle's awfully heavy, you know.'

'Serves you right for being such a great fat oaf,' said
Parker, The Pride of the Third (The Sludgethorpe Walton-
ians' Third Division Second Reserves). 'You'll just have to
keep up as best you can.'

'Suit yourself,' puffed McGinty, 'but I do have all the pop
in this shoulder bag.'

The procession skidded to a halt as the other two leapt on
the Owl of the Saloon.

'Ouch. Yaroo! Leggo, you cads!'

'There you are, McGinty, old prune. Your bag's a lot lighter now. Mac and I will look after the pop until we get to our pitch. You'd only be swigging it while our backs were turned, anyway.'

Snuffling into his balaclava, McGinty lurched disconsolately behind as his two friends stepped lightly and speedily along the towpath.

'I'll get my own back on you rotters,' he muttered. 'Just you see if I don't.'

By the time McGinty caught up, the others had already settled down at the bank, tackled up and cast out.

'That's a bit off,' puffed the Fat One. 'You've snitched the best two spots and left me with Gudgeons' Graveyard again. Three weeks running you've done that. What about the old motto: "Share and share alike"? Or "All for one and one for all"?'

'We're living up to the other mottos,' said Mac. ' "To each his own". And "Last one here's a sissy".'

'Then take that, you cads!' yelled McGinty, tipping a handful of maggots down each of their necks and stamping on their breadpaste before fleeing back down the towpath. 'I'm fishing over here, anyway. We'll see who gets the most.'

Our priceless pair didn't do too well for the first hour; in fact they caught nothing. Matters were not made much better by McGinty's thundering up and down in laps of honour for the two gudgeon which had somehow found their way onto his hook.

'Stop that, you great fat twit!' shouted Parker. 'You're putting all the fish down!'

'Yah boo sucks!' McGinty shouted back. 'Serves you right! And sticks and stones may break my -'

'Aw, shaddap!'

Later, when the pair took out the pop and pulled at the rings on the cans, McGinty realised he would have to make his peace.

'Bygones be bygones, chaps?' he asked hesitantly, shuffling cautiously nearer. 'Pax, and all that? Do you think I could have some of that pop? I did chip in for it, after all.'

'Righto, old chap,' said Parker, winking slyly at Mad Mac. 'Forgive and forget. Play up and play the game, eh?'

As McGinty tilted back his head and raised the can to his

parched lips, oblivious for the moment of his surroundings, Parker lifted up the Fat One's anorak and pulled out the waistband of his outsize trousers, allowing Mad Mac to tip a bait can of cold canal water down into the cavernous gulf.

'Yaroo!' yelled McGinty, leaping up and down the towpath with watering eyes. 'You bounders! You absolute rotters! It's all run down into my wellies!'

The fleet-footed pair easily dodged the rod rest with which McGinty tried to belabour them. At last he gave up, out of breath, and peace descended once more upon the canal.

'I've got this new catapult,' said Mac. 'Isn't it a beauty? I can drop bait onto a 10p piece at 30 yards with this. From here I could hit that duck right on the –'

'A bit naughty,' said Parker. 'Our feathered friends and all that. Why don't you try for something bigger?'

'Such as?' said Mac, then followed Parker's gaze to where McGinty was sulking, way down the bank.

There was a scream as the ball of soggy groundbait, liberally laced with maggots, hit McGinty on the ear with a loud *splat*!

'That's done it, you chaps!' yelled McGinty. 'Just for that I'm packing up and going to the tuckshop.'

'Do that then!' shouted the pair. 'And give us a bit of peace. Great big crybaby!'

The Owl of the Saloon lumbered off to the old-world tuckshop with its sign of the Three Horseshoes, and left our heroes to their fishing. Nothing happened, however: the commotion had obviously scared away every fish on the stretch.

So they, too, packed up and made for the tuckshop.

'Your turn to get them in,' said Parker.

'Impossible, old chap,' said Mac. 'I was banking on the receipt of a Girocheque, which for some unfathomable reason has failed to turn up.'

'Well, I'm skint. The milkman caught me at home again yesterday.'

'I've got it!' said Mac. 'McGinty! He's come up on the pools! Had a postal order from Littlewoods yesterday.'

The pair marched cheerily into the tuckshop and approached the Owl, who was staring morosely into his half-empty glass.

'Hello, old chum!' they cried. 'What jolly fun we've had

119

this morning, eh? And just in case there's been any slight misunderstanding, let's sink our differences in a glass or two of pop.'

'You can sink what you like,' said McGinty. 'So long as you're paying. If you're after my postal order, you might like to know it was only for £1.80. And I've just supped it.'

It's not true that big boys don't cry...

33

The Way That You Say It

I think I've found out what's wrong with Mad Mac. Or I
think I've found out why we have difficulty in com-
municating. It's the Weddell Seal Effect.

Scientists have discovered that Weddell seals living on
opposite sides of the Antarctic use different dialects. As do
Mac and I. They have difficulty in understanding each
other. As do Mac and I. We're the same species, roughly
speaking, but he comes from Deepest Gateshead and I from
Darkest Manchester.

One lot of Weddell seals uses more sounds than the other.
That's Mac, all right. He uses more sounds than anybody.
The seals use mirror-image sounds, too, in which the first
phrase is slowed down and the second phrase speeded up.
That's Mac when he says, slowing down: 'I'd love to buy
you a pint.' Then, speeding up: 'But I haven't got any
money.'

In fact he doesn't say quite that. He says, 'I haven't got
any money, but.' Which is a Geordie-type mirror image of
normal speech.

This gets confusing when we're discussing the Floating
Fiver.

'You owe me a fiver,' I say.

'I owe you a fiver, but,' says Mac.

'What you're really trying to say is, "But I owe you a
fiver".'

'Do you? Thanks, ol' buddy. I'll take it now if you've got
it, but.'

*   *   *

Other scientists have been doing research into what our ears actually hear, and how the brain can misinterpret signals. That's another trouble with Mac. The signals reach his ears, but somehow get scrambled along the way.

'I'm trying out a new float,' say I, during a break in the pub. 'A waggler. What's yours?'

'A pint of best, ol' buddy.'

Time passes.

'I'm pulling in some lovely gudgeon down there. What are you having?'

'Another pint of best. Ta, but.'

Comes the shout of Last Orders and panic sets in. Leading to a diminution of the old Parker politeness.

'Your turn, you cadging toad.'

'One for the road? Just a Scotch, ol' buddy. Large one, if you can spring it, but.'

...Another peculiarity of Geordie speech is the ability to break bad news gently, which comes of centuries of border warfare in the old days: getting thumped first by the Scots and then by the Yorkies, occasionally by the Lankies and anybody else passing through.

'How's that reel I lent you?' I asked.

'Just fine,' said Mac. 'I'm using my own at the moment, but.'

'Right. Let's have mine back, then. Cost a lot of money, that did.'

'Glad to, ol' buddy. Small snag, but.'

'What do you mean, small snag? I thought you said the reel was fine.'

'Oh, aye. In perfect working order. The last time I saw it. And that.'

'The last time you saw it?'

'Aye, but.'

'And when was that?'

'Just before it fell in the watter.'

* * *

Mac and I have been puzzled for years by the way that Big McGinty, who causes far more havoc on the bank than the average rhino, always gets away unscathed. While Mac and I, in trying to help him out, tend to emerge severely scathed.

The penny's just dropped. A survey of British speech patterns shows that if you talk with a posh accent – which McGinty can put on very well in moments of crisis – people tend to look upon you as a well-educated, respectable, responsible, upright and sober citizen.

The classic example was the Great Lock Gate Disaster. McGinty, in his hurry to get to the *Thwarted Ferret* from the other side of the canal, sprinted across the lock. Or he tried to. He'd only sprinted halfway across when he slipped and did a 19-stone bellyflop which disturbed the stretch for a hundred yards. This brought some naughty words and very rude gestures from the lads whose keepnets and terminal tackle suffered from the tidal wave.

Mac and I formed a semi-human chain to haul McGinty to the pubside bank. There we were met by a very steamy bailiff person, demanding to know what we thought we were a-doing of, ruining the fishing for the paying customers.

Explanations from the two of us met with even fiercer response. Then McGinty stopped spluttering and spoke up:

'Terribly sorry, old chap,' he wheezed. 'Knee gave way. Old wound. Always acts up in this weather. Hope I've not put you to any inconvenience. Any expense...naturally... my account...'

'Never you mind, sir,' said the bailiff, calming down and drooling respect. 'Just you get yourself to the *Thwarted Ferret* and dry off. Get something warm down you to keep off the chill. Can't be too careful, I always say.'

As Mac and I lugged McGinty to his feet and turned him in the direction of the pub, the bailiff's expression changed again.

'Just a minute,' he said, sternly. 'You two! Don't think I've forgotten this. I'll keep an eye out in future!'

Aye, but...

34

Well, I'll be Bugged

Amazing what people get up to these days. I saw some ads recently for business espionage equipment: aids to spying on your deadly rival.

There are tiny electronic bugs you can put in his phone; little microphones you can stick under his desk, or even to the bottom of his briefcase. There's another gadget you can stick in your earhole to pick up the transmissions, plus a little tape recorder to get it all down.

Just in case you fail to stick anything on his briefcase, there's a tiny directional mike which can eavesdrop on conversations yards away. Weeny telescopes so that you can read any document he's incautious enough to pull out in public. And, should you get close enough, a camera built into a cigarette lighter.

Just to show their impartiality, the manufacturers also offer anti-espionage devices: bug detectors, microphone scramblers and the like. Plus something which gives the alarm if any naughty person should slip explosives into your natty executive case. There were no ads for explosives, but perhaps if you asked nicely...

I hope the idea never spreads to the match scene. There's enough aggro there already without bugs in your basket or bangers in your breadpaste. Let's just be thankful that the average match scene has enough natural obstacles to defeat even the most sophisticated electronic espionage.

Take those two blokes over at the bar, deep in argument. Bound to be discussing the baits and tactics for the needle match the following day. Tune in with your directional microphone and find out what's causing the controversy:

'It's *your* round, I tell you.'

'Never! I got the last one.'

'Right. But you still owe me one from last night.'

'I never do. I bought you one just before closing time.'

'Yes, but what with? That fiver I lent you. Which reminds me ...'

*   *   *

Little use bugging a basket, certainly not a wicker one. All you'd get from that would be creaks as the owner settled down, followed by some strange noises-off as his breakfast settled down.

Conversation picked up inside a metal box would be drowned by the echo-chamber effect as it was banged down on the bank or tripped over. You might stand a chance when the lid was opened, if it were not for the creaking of the hinges and the *boings*! and *kerlangs*! as the bottles of light ale were lifted out.

*   *   *

You certainly wouldn't get much change from eaves-dropping on a Yorkshire match team's conversation. It's a peculiarity of Yorkies that they seldom finish a sentence. They don't like to waste words, possibly because of their natural thrift. So you'd get something like:

'Mornin', Jim. What d'yer reckon?'

'No sweat. Providing I can get a peg near t' ...'

'Near t' ...? Nay, lad. Yer'd be better off wi' one down t' ...'

'Down t' ...? Give over. Didn't yer know about factory? Last week it tipped in gallons o' ...'

'Oh 'eck. I didn't know that. Gallons o' ...? So what're you ...?'

'I'm usin' some o' them ...'

'Some o' *them*, eh? I tried 'em last week. No chance. I've switched to ...'

'That's all very well, but t' real secret's in t' groundbait. I've dosed mine wi' ...'

'Ave yer now? Well that should liven 'em up a bit. But fer my money on this stretch, there's nowt like a good dollop o' ...'

125

Yerss... With the Yorkies, you'd be better off taking a course in extrasensory perception.

*   *   *

Keep it simple. Try using your Super Snooper miniature telescope. See that lad down the bank, reading some obviously confidential document as he sits watching for a twitch? Bound to be secret plans for the match which he is under oath to eat as soon as he's read. Focus over his shoulder and discover the deadly secrets.

Marvellous, these little telescopes. You can even read the number at the top of the page. That's it, coming into focus now: *Page Three*. And what's that picture underneath? Looks like... yes, it is - a smiling young lady person with no clothes on. In this weather.

And what's it say in those capital letters?:

SHE MAY BE AN ANGLER'S DAUGHTER
BUT SHE WON'T SWALLOW ANY OLD LINE

A specialist's code, no doubt. It's nice to know that *somebody* is taking his fishing seriously...

35

Go Strong With Pongg!

Anglers, because of their sheer numbers, carry a very hefty political clout. It's just a pity they don't use it properly; organise themselves as a challenge to the other political parties; produce a manifesto which puts angling first and last, and which would attract the vote of every decent, honest, upright, fair-minded, democratic, freedom-loving Brother of the Angle. And his missis, if she knows what's good for her.

Into the breach, filling the vacuum, not to mention a long felt want, is PONGG, the Piscators' Organisation for Nitty Gritty Government, the party formed by anglers, of anglers and for anglers. *PONGG for One and PONGG for All*, is the slogan. The party has been a bit late coming out with its manifesto on account of Mad Mac losing the pencil, but it's all ready now.

Contents of the manifesto were approved only last night in a meeting of the party's Executive Committee in the phone box outside the *Boot and Slipper*. That is to say two of the Executive Committee, Mac and myself, were able to get into the phone box. McGinty had to hold a one-man overflow meeting outside.

Right, then, brothers. What does PONGG promise you?

First of all, a Minister for Angling. Either me or Mad Mac, depending on who loses the toss for Prime Minister. With a junior minister to take care of minority sports such as ludo and football hooliganism.

The Min. for Ang. will have total powers to implement the most immediate reforms.

Foremost among these will be the provision of duty-free

draught bitter for card-carrying anglers, and the granting of 24-hour licences to fishing pubs. Abuse of such privileges will be safeguarded against by strict penalties for non-anglers, such as having to buy drinks all round.

Anglers will be exempt from Income Tax. Fishing tackle and bait will be exempt from VAT and strict limits imposed on wholesale and retail profit margins.

All fishing in the British Isles will be free. Except to wealthy foreign tourists, in which case it will be prohibitive. Maintenance of waters will be financed by levies on such anti-angling organisations as power boat manufacturers and teetotallers.

Maggot farmers and worm breeders will be granted subsidies similar to those enjoyed by agricultural-type farmers. Production will be strictly controlled so as not to result in a maggie mountain or a lob jam, which might result in flogging off the surplus at knockdown prices behind the Iron Curtain or dumping it in the Grand Union Canal.

Money will be made available for research into breeding bigger maggies and dafter fish.

Anglers will be granted a three-day working week, with no loss of pay, and a four-hour lunch break.

Imperial weights and measures will be restored on the grounds that nobody's yet got the hang of the metric ones. Who knows how much a 1.7 kilogramme chub weighs? Or how many maggies in a demilitre? And how many heart attacks have been caused by anglers being told that the next pub is 3.5 kilometres away?

So much for PONGG's economic policies. What of the social ones, I hear you asking.

Water skiing will be banned and water-skiers ordered to put in such forms of community service as mucking out canals drained for cleaning and doing the odd stint down the salt mines. An amnesty will be declared for match stewards after the completion of terms of similar service.

The angling scene will change as surplus hot water from power stations and hot air from Westminster is used to heat canals and reservoirs to a temperature amenable to tropical fish. A few mahseers and Nile perch should shake up the old rod-caught records a bit. Salt mined by the former water-skiers will be used to salinate chosen reservoirs so that we can chuck in the odd white shark.

Early in the legislation will come the Anti-Discrimination Act. ADA, as it will be known, will ensure that no angler is discriminated against by publicans, bus conductors, bank managers and the like on account of ponging, carrying a mountain of gear or being permanently skint.

There will be grants for day release courses in the arts of Creative Imagination and Verbal Fabrication (i.e. fibbing) so that anglers can make their stories sound (a) convincing, (b) interesting or (c) hilarious. Heavy penalties will be introduced for audiences who do not either gasp in amazement or burst into hysterical laughter, depending on whether the stories are supposed to be serious or funny.

The angler's domestic circumstances will be dealt with by the Battered Anglers Act. Anglers who are severely beaten by their wives on account of coming home late or falling about, or in any similar condition inseparable from the Noble Art, will be able to take refuge in Purpose Built Sanctuaries - PUBS, for short - until the swellings go down. Wives found guilty of battery will be sentenced to be nice to the lad for at least six months on pain of losing their Anglers' Spouses' Unsocial Hours Allowance.

The House of Lords will be given a bit of tone by the elevation to the Peerage of selected anglers of proven intelligence, wit and wisdom, i.e. me, Mad Mac and Big McGinty.

The health of anglers will be given special consideration, expecially that of Senior Citizen anglers who are finding the old rheumatics setting in on account of sitting so long on damp banks and leaning so long on damp bars. Senior anglers remember; even if you're at death's door, PONGG will pull you through.

Ah, yes. PONGG is but a small movement as yet. A tight-knit bunch, as you might say. A bunch of tighter nits you've yet to meet. But once we're in power any such subversive comments will be severely dealt with. Salt mines for you, woman, if you're not careful. (Ouch! No need for that.)

So that's it folks. When you place your vote at the next General Election, remember: You Can't Go Wrong If You Vote For PONGG!!!

36

The Best Policy

It comes to something when fiddling is so rife that match
fishing authorities are having to use lie detectors at the
weigh-in.

It's not happening in Britain, of course. Like as if. But lie-
detecting is now standard practice in Texas, where big
money sea matches are being infiltrated by unprincipled
lads who stock up their bilges with big fish before the
match and add them to their catch.

The Texas Bass Association noticed some strange
happenings when their modest trophies were replaced by
big money prizes ranging from 30,000 to 100,000 dollars.
All of a sudden, catches soared to impossible proportions.
After allowing for the extra incentive, there was no way
that even the Lone Star State could produce so many
angling wizards all of a sudden.

'They're coming out of the woodwork,' said a Fishing and
Wildlife Department official. 'It's the big bucks that attract
them.'

So anyone with a suspiciously large catch is now asked to
take a lie detector test before the dibs are handed over.
Already a Grand Jury has been convened to hear
testimony about two brothers who collected 65,000 dollars
in prize money, then were disqualified after the lie detector
blew a couple of gaskets.

And the authorities are on the trail of a fish-smuggling
ring, stretching right through Texas, Louisiana, Arkansas
and Florida, which they reckon has won up to 250,000
dollars illegally by slipping anglers the extra weight they
need for first prize.

Although cheating does happen in Britain, it's unlikely to reach the epidemic proportions of Texas. And it's doubtful if the lie detector would ever replace the old-fashioned clogging behind the clubhouse. But in case it does, it's as well to be prepared.

Lie detectors are not infallible, you see. They can be affected by factors other than common-or-garden fibbing. Somebody who is totally innocent, but nervous or confused, could set the detector off. Somebody who is as guilty as sin, but cool as a cucumber, could walk away with profuse apologies ringing in his ears and reverberating off his brass neck.

Emotional tension is all the detector can register, and there are three main ways of doing this: by changes in blood pressure, the rate of breathing, or by changes in the electrical resistance of the skin. The machines which register these changes – and it's as well to know about them in case the things do appear over here – are:

The *sphygmomanometer* – and if you can say that you're a better man than I am – is the detector that works on blood pressure. Even the preliminary question – 'Do you know what this is?' – can send your blood pressure through the roof as you try to pronounce it. Especially if you've not put your teeth in: you can lose points for splashing.

When it's explained to you that this, you ignorant twit, is a sphygmomanometer, it's no use trying to make light of it by saying, 'Oh, yes. I had one of those but the wheels fell off.' Nobody laffs. Your joke, such as it was, has died the death. You are stricken by the dreaded Club Comic's Curse, wishing you could follow the joke into oblivion, and up goes the blood pressure again.

Anger, too, can make your blood pressure rise. So if you get worked up by the aspersions being cast upon you, or the interrogator hits you with a sockful of ripe rubby dubby, you are once more branded as a fibber.

The *pneumograph* records changes in your breathing. Changes in this can be brought about by many other things besides guilt, such as whether you're gasping for a fag, thinking impure thoughts about Dolly Parton, or your interrogator is shaking hands with your neck as an aid to total recall.

A *psychogalvanometer* records changes in the electrical resistance of the skin, caused by chemical changes on the

surface resulting from mental activity. Sweating, in plain English.

This detector shows the best results on intelligent and emotional characters. So if you're as thick as two short planks and only get upset when Man United goes down, you could sit plugged in all day without a flicker.

But if you're at all sensitive, nobody need even so much as mention fish to get the needle waving wildly all over the place. Sheer fright can do it, brought on by buzzwords such as 'Inland Revenue', 'Drink up please – well past time', 'Mother-in-law' and 'Margaret Thatcher'.

* * *

Anyway, that's what you're in for if British match fishing ever gets tainted by filthy lucre to the extent of the goings-on in Texas. And remember that the lie detector isn't the end of it: you can still get caught out by an incautious remark.

As witness the angler who sat strapped to the detector for an hour and stood up to the most rigorous questioning and personal abuse without a single twitch from the machine.

'You're free to go now,' said the interrogator. 'Sorry to put you through all that, but you'll be happy to know you can leave this room without a stain on your character.'

'Thanks very much,' said the angler. 'Just one thing. I've got another match next week. Could I have the fish back...?'

37

Making Your Peace

Christmas comes but once a year. (End of Great Thought.)
But when it comes it does not always bring Good Cheer,
especially among fishing families, where the Pursuit of the
Angle and the odd extra pint can lead to some unfortunate
misunderstandings, not to mention the raking up of all the
transgressions over the past twelve months.

So this time I'd like you to remember that Christmas time
is Family time. Let's keep it jolly. Let's keep it peaceful.
And it'll be mainly up to you: you've not got to mess
Christmas up again like you did last year. (How did I
know? Just psychic, that's all.)

Start your Christmas peace efforts early, making up to
the family for any little misunderstandings of the past
year.

Apologise to the lads in the family for borrowing their
tackle. It's newer than yours, in better condition, and
without it you'd never have achieved the position you did in
your club's individual matchweight table. Yes, without
their tackle, you could well have come bottom. Instead of
which you came second. From bottom.

Return all the tackle, all that you can find, so that they've
got it for their own Christmas fishing. Promise to repair the
bent floats, silted-up reels and shredded keep nets as soon
as you've got a second. Then keep out of their way.

Apologise to the girls, too. To the little ones, for digging
up their garden flower patches in a desperate search for
worms. To the bigger ones, for nicking their nail varnish to
liven up your floats. And for throwing out those boyfriends
whose interests didn't run to fishing and boozing.

Say you're sorry to the father-in-law for what you said when he dropped you right in it. That night you and he got back very late, tired and emotional, and you told the wife there had been a special emergency meeting of the club welfare committee to discuss a matter of the gravest importance. Life and death. And that old twit announced what a great time you'd both had, supping after hours at the *Cock and Bottle*.

Make your peace with the mother-in-law, too. You didn't really mean those things you said about her last January. And February. And March. And... All in jest, it was. She's not really a two-faced, interfering old bat. Nor a scheming, conniving, trouble-making ratbag. And certainly not a fat, ugly old blatherskite who wouldn't be allowed to haunt a house in case she frightened the ghosts.

What's that? She'd forgotten that last bit? Oh, 'eck...

Make your peace with the pets, too, for stealing their tins of nourishing, vitamin-enriched doggy/moggy food to use as bait, leaving them with nothing for it but to go busking round the neighbours.

And forgive them their trespasses. The dog, for scoffing most of your groundbait when your back was turned. The cat, for making off with those fresh herrings you intended to go piking with.

Apologise even to the budgie, to whom you had to turn for droppings as a groundbait additive after the bloke next door sold his pigeons. And whose premature demise you almost caused by feeding it birdseed soaked in castor oil.

Don't forget the neighbours. They're sort of family, after all, and they've had plenty to put up with. Wakened by your falling over the milk bottles as you left on your dawn fishing trips. And falling over them again as you returned late at night. Not to mention your midnight renditions of *Delilah* after a hard evening at the club social. Nor the pongs from your maggot breeding projects and the binful of rubby dubby ripening in the shed.

Above all, make your peace with the wife. The little woman who has put up with you for yet another year, whose life has been made little short of horrific by the discovery of maggots in the fridge, pike in the bath, and unconscious mates snoring behind the settee. Whose culinary efforts have been thwarted time after time by the discovery that the larder has been cleaned out of beans,

135

luncheon meat, frankfurters, cheese, cocoa and custard powder.

Christmas Day, especially, you are not to mess up again. No matter what time the pubs close or the match finishes, let's have you home in time for Christmas dinner. No lurching in half an hour after everybody's sat down, demanding to know why they're all looking daggers at you. And no dragging home a little friend you've found abandoned in the pub.

Little friends are abandoned in pubs every Christmas. Leave 'em there. There's often a good reason for their being abandoned, as you no doubt discovered when last year's little friend polished off everything from turkey to pud, settled in your favourite chair, took his boots off, lit one of your cigars and complained about the quality of the brandy.

* * *

Let's get back to the wife. You've made your peace. You're going to be a good lad from now on, cross your heart and hope to die. And you're going to set the seal on your resolution by buying her a proper present this year. A present she'll like and can use; not the usual litre bottle of Scotch or set of floats.

I've done Dearly Beloved really proud. Bought her a mixer, a grinder and a blender for the kitchen. She's always fancied those, and this year I thought what the hell. Last of the big spenders, me.

So she'll be able to play with them straightaway on Christmas morning, I've got them all ready: put the plugs on and tested them out. I must say that all three of them work superbly. Should you be thinking of buying the same, I can thoroughly recommend them.

The mixer. A couple of minutes with that and you've got some beautifully textured dough bait, with the high protein additives mixed evenly all the way through.

The grinder. How smoothly it reduces wheat and oats to use as fine groundbait. How quickly it chops down a handful of worms into bite-sized pieces for the fishes' little rosebud mouths.

And the blender. Warm water, custard powder, any kind of flavouring essence, and in seconds you've got a beaker full of liquid gold to squidge into the groundbait.

Pardon? No, I've been testing them, that's all. I washed them out properly, dried them, and put them back in the boxes. I wouldn't dream of using them regularly for preparing bait. Not until after Christmas. Not until things are – how can I put it? – a bit more peaceful.

38

For Services Rendered

The New Year's Honours List has got a bit boring of recent
years. Few surprises, and the rewards going for services to
the most obvious causes.

It's time that some more titles were dished out for
services to angling. It is, after all, the biggest participant
sport in Britain, and does far less harm to innocent
bystanders than most of the others. Unless you're standing
too close to Mad Mac or Big McGinty.

My idea is not to give the awards to anglers, but to the
women behind them. They're the ones who have to put up
with all the muck and mess back home, all the steaming
clothes strewn across the floor after a match, all the
moaning and groaning after a bad result, and all the
falling about after a sorrows-drowning session.

It is my privilege to spend my spare time in the company
of some of the country's top anglers. A tight-knit bunch,
they are. (Dearly Beloved reckons she's never known a
bunch of tighter nits.)

Ace anglers they may be, but they wouldn't be where they
are today without the patience, forbearance, help and
encouragement of their Nearest and Dearest. So never
mind the tight nits: it's their long suffering wives I'm going
to nominate for the next New Year's Honours:

Missis Doc Thumper. For turning out as deckhand in all
weathers when Doc goes charging off downriver in his
boat. For not screaming as Doc, with his customary navi-
gational skill, heads at top speed for the edge of a weir. And
for eating the mixed grills which Doc insists on cooking
aboard the boat. Ducks have been known to sink after

scoffing Doc's fried bread. What it does to the human digestive system has not been fully researched, but it definitely is in breach of several clauses of the Geneva Convention.

Missis Mad Mac. For putting up with Mac's monetarist policies, i.e. nicking a fiver every week, regular as clockwork, out of the housekeeping. And for putting up with Mac's monumental enthusiams. Every week he has a new craze, invents a new piece of tackle, concocts another sure-fire killer-diller groundbait. And leaves a hell of a mess behind him. Missis Mac has never had a piece of knitting yet that wasn't held up halfway because the wool had been nicked for Mac's new improved Superduper Dippy Dapper.

And for putting up with Mac's feet. I don't know what it is about his feet, but they should carry a Government Health Warning. Once they've been in his wellies for ten minutes, they go right off. Anybody who goes nightfishing with Mac must insist that he keeps his wellies on inside the tent. If he takes them off, you're dead.

Missis Big McGinty. For clearing up the wreckage after him as he lumbers around the house, especially if he's come back from the water a bit tired and emotional. It's not that he deliberately breaks things; just that anything he picks up falls to pieces, anything he leans on collapses, anything he sits on crumples into dust. He's the only bloke I know who buys six fishing baskets a year.

Missis McGinty is nominated also for shivering through the night on account of McGinty's fresh air fetish. In the depths of winter he insists on sleeping with the windows wide open. Icicles, he reckons, are all in the mind. He never feels the cold, perhaps because of his 19 stone of insulation or more likely because he nicks all the bedclothes.

Missus Cousin Jim from Leeds. The lovely Philomena. Who copes with the effects of Jim's encounters with animals on the bank. Cows falling on him; runaway horses dragging him up hill and down dale, mice nesting in his wellies and objecting strongly to being disturbed. That kind of thing. She's always there when Jim is carried back from the water, ready with a mug of steaming hot tea, first aid kit and splints.

Missis Mitch. For collecting Mitch from the low stone wall outside the station, which for some reason is where he always finishes up after a hard-fought away match. Mitch is always in a curious condition - i.e. unconscious and horizontal - brought about by killing the pain after a disastrous result, or celebrating after a glorious victory.

After dragging Mitch off the wall and shoving him into the car, she then has to go back and collect his tackle, which is strewn all the way from Platform 2, and help the porter sweep the maggots from the steps.

Dearly Beloved. I'd love to nominate her, but it might seem like favouritism. After all, she doesn't have a lot to put up with. A nicer, tidier, more considerate little feller than her husband, you couldn't wish to –

The large lump rising slowly on the back of my head is possibly connected with the frying pan in her hand. Could it have been something I said ... ?

39

Deed-A-Day Cliffie

Among this New Year's resolutions is to Do A Good Deed Every Day.

I must admit that I was inspired by Doc Thumper, whose motto this is, year in, year out. He does so many good deeds all over the place that sometimes people get a bit fed up with it.

Let him see an old lady standing on the pavement, and instantly she's helped across the road. On the other side, she explains that she was only standing on the pavement to get her breath back.

At least, with Doc's Old-World charm and bedside manner, there's always a happy ending. When I try it, I always seem to end up in bother.

Hardly had the New Year got under way than I espied an old lady standing at some traffic lights with two big bags of shopping at her feet.

'Allow me, dear lady,' I cried, hoisting up her two bags of goodies.

'Go away, you silly mugger!' she cried. (I think that was what she cried.) And gave me one with her brolly.

Nothing daunted, if you'll excuse the cliché, I espied another old lady standing near some roadworks past which a huge juggernaut had just thundered. Holding a dog lead, she was, and looking ever so distraught. There was no sign of whatever had been on the other end of the lead.

'Gad!' I thought. 'Her poor little doggie-pog has been flattened by that speeding juggernaut. I shall dash over and comfort her.'

Over I dashed. Comfort flashing from every pore.

'I'm so terribly sorry about your little dog,' I said. 'Is there anything I can do?'

'Yes,' she said. 'Go away. Can't you see he's busy?'

There at her feet, hidden by the roadworks, was the doggie-pog. Confidently cocking its leg up at a flashing lamp thoughtfully provided by the Council.

So I was sorely tempted t'other day to give a negative response (ie., 'Get knotted') to the old chap who approached the swim I was trying for the first time.

'Good morning, young man,' he piped in a feeble treble. 'Are they biting well today?'

'Furiously,' I said. Lying furiously. I'd not had a twitch all morning.

'Oh... In which case, I won't bother you. So nice to see somebody catching...'

'No, just a minute,' I said. 'What's up?'

'It's only that I usually fish this swim. It's quite dry on this bit of the bank, and being on a bend it's out of the wind. At my age, I can't sit just anywhere. You don't realise how lucky you –'

'Come in, me old son,' I said. 'I can move downstream a bit. No probs.'

I wasn't being noble. *That* swim he was welcome to.

I helped the old boy down the bank, helped him to set his stall out, moved further downstream and left him to it.

All was silence. At least, from my new swim. From the one I'd just handed over came cries from th'owd feller of: 'Oh! She's a beauty!'; 'Gotcha!' and 'By Jove, young man – you weren't telling a lie were you? They *are* biting furiously.'

Mutter, mutter. Curse, curse.

At the end of the morning I packed up with just enough fish to fill a tea strainer. And was therefore not too kindly disposed towards the appeal from the next swim:

'Excuse me, young sir. Would you mind helping me to pack up?'

But remembering my resolution, especially after the 'young sir' bit, I went over.

'It's the keepnet I have trouble with,' said the old lad. 'My back, you know. Quite heavy, these things.'

I hauled out the keepnet. He was right. It *was* heavy.

'Not bad for an old 'un, eh?' he quavered. 'Let's see,

now ... Six bream ... Nine decent roach – or are they chub, young feller-me-lad? My eyes aren't what they were ... Five perch – nice ones... About a dozen bleak...'

After putting the fish back, and pausing only for the green flush to disappear from my finely chiselled countenance, I helped the old boy with his gear to a pub. He was obviously a regular from the way he laid claim to the best seat near the fire and addressed the barmaid as 'Sweetie'.

'What are you having?' I asked, keeping up the good-deed routine.

'Most kind,' said the old boy. 'A pint of best, please.'

He burbled on a bit about the old days on the river and fairly soon drained his pint.

'What are you having, young sir?' he said. 'Once I can get out of this chair, that is. Seem to be having a bit of trouble with the old joints these days.'

'Don't worry,' I said. 'Allow me. My treat.'

He shifted that pint and another before he stopped rabbiting and decided it was time to go. Good-deeding to the end, I moved the table out of his way and helped him to the door.

'Bye, Sweetie!' he called to the barmaid.

'Bye,' she said. And then, 'Where's your father this week?'

Father? She must be joking. But no.

'He's a fair weather fisherman,' said the old lad. 'Besides, he's too mean these days to take me to a pub. Spends all the time at home with his video.'

Thank God for that, I thought. *Father*. With two of 'em to buy ale for, after their nicking the swim and putting me to shame with their catches, they would have put a severe strain on the Good Deed ethic.

So count your blessings, Parker, I thought. Quit while you're still ahead. *Father*. I ask you. At home with the video. Bet you any money he's watching *Emmanuelle*...

40

Fit to Bust

'You're not fit to be let out,' said Dearly Beloved. 'What *am* I going to do with you.'

'You might have some sympathy, for a start,' I said, from my recumbent and painful posture on the settee. 'And may I remind you that I sustained these injuries – from which I may possibly die – *before* I went to the pub, not after.'

'I wouldn't care,' she said. 'But it's every year at this time. Regular as clockwork.'

She was right. Every year, just as I think I'm safe from the Ding Dong Merrilys and Ringing in the New, I do myself a mischief by falling down something, off something or into something. Sustaining damage to my coccyx (look it up), which gives me a funny walk; or to my casting arm, which plays hell with the old flex and flick.

This year, as the casualty officer confirmed, I'd got the winning double; a bruised bone in the bum and a broken finger in the right hand.

It happened on a slippery bit of the Grand Union towpath; black ice, I shouldn't wonder. Mad Mac and Big McGinty carried me into the pub to discuss my case and the best course of action to take. It took them until closing time to reach the conclusion that I was not at all well. Good job I wasn't bleeding to death.

I couldn't keep getting up and down in the pub, on account of my coccyx, and I couldn't get my hand into my back pocket on account of the finger, which by now was doing a good imitation of a purple frankfurter.

'On me, ol' buddy,' said Mac. 'Just stay there and I'll get them in.'

'Don't know what all the fuss is about,' said McGinty. 'Pain is all in the mind. Remember when I fell off the coach after that away match? I just carried on as if nothing had happened. It wasn't until six months later that the quack told me I'd had a hairline fracture of the skull. Never did me any harm. Doctors! What do *they* know?'

It is a proven fact that McGinty has been clinically barmy ever since, but I let it pass.

* * *

The noble lads got me home and explained the situation to Dearly Beloved.

'Bring him in,' she said, 'and I'll put the kettle on for a cup of tea.'

'Tea?' I croaked. 'I've got a battered bum, a broken finger, I'm coming out in bruises all over and I've pulled almost every muscle in my body. What the hell do I have to do to get a Scotch?'

'Trust you,' she said. 'Any excuse.'

Still, bless her, she got out the Scotch. To which Mac and McGinty, unmindful of the fact that I was the injured party, helped themselves in generous measures.

'Gad, I needed that,' said Mac, slurping down his first. 'After what we've been through.'

He and McGinty launched into accounts of the incident which sounded as if they'd struggled for days through snowbound Alpine passes to rescue a stricken comrade, instead of just picking me off the towpath and frog-marching me to the pub.

'...Anyway, thanks very much for looking after him, lads,' said Dearly Beloved, as Mac was about to launch on his fourth dramatic recital. 'But don't let us detain you.'

'Shucks, it's nothing,' said Mac, peering at the bottom of his empty glass. 'Our ol' buddy. Least we could do.'

'I'm afraid there's no Scotch left,' said Dearly Beloved. 'You've finished it.'

'Dear me,' said Mac. 'Is that the time?'

'Just one thing,' I said from my prone position. 'Where's my tackle?'

'Left it with the landlord,' said Mac. 'As security for the drinks I put on the slate. Didn't like to tell you that I was temporarily financially embarrassed. And that McGinty was in the same state, it being the time of year. Anyway, the landlord said he'd be glad to raffle it off.'

'Raffle it off? What the hell for?'

'Only should your angling days prove to be over, ol' buddy. God forbid. Help to defray expenses...'

'I'll defray you!' I squawked, lurching to my feet with an effort that brought tears to my eyes.

'Must fly,' said Mac, shooting through the door with McGinty lumbering hard on his heels.

* * *

What is life like for a shattered angler, with a grotty botty and a duffy digit? Can things ever be the same again? Or are our hero's angling days gone for good? Will his tackle be raffled by a mercenary landlord to defray expenses on account of Mad Mac's temporary (for which read permanent) financial embarrassment?

I'll report back in the next chapter. Should I be spared...

41

Torque Me Out Of It

'Yerss... You've broken your middle finger all right,' said
the hospital casualty officer cheerily, as he peered at the X-
rays. 'Just go over there to Nurse for treatment.'

'Thanks,' I said. 'May I see the X-rays?'

Nurse had to treat me first for coming over all funny. It's
a weird feeling, seeing your own skeleton, especially when
one of the bones has a diagonal crack all the way down it.
The nurse then carried out the complicated and highly
skilled treatment for a busted finger: she taped it to the next
one with two bits of sticking plaster. I knew things were
tight in the National Health Service, but whatever
happened to splints?

The first job, the following weekend, was to settle up with
the landlord and recover my tackle from the boozer. He
seemed disappointed to see me: obviously the raffle value of
the tackle was more than Mac had spent on drinks. Not a
lot, though: especially when you added on the three packets
of salt and vinegar and 20 filter tips that Mac had bunged
on the slate while he was at it.

Almost immediately I started to learn the perils of
angling with a duff digit. I swung the basket up to my
shoulder, the strap in the crook of my right thumb as is my
wont, and – Aaaargh!

'Careful,' said the landlord. 'Torque, that is.'

'I never said a word. Apart from "Aaaargh!"'

'No – *torque*. Twisting action caused through tension in
the muscles. Goes all through your hand. Engineering
term. I learned about it when I was a fitter in the RAF.
When I was out in Suez...'

'Thanks,' I said. 'I'll remember that.' And máde my exit, not wishing to be bogged down in the landlord's war memoirs. And I'm sure he wouldn't have been interested in my own memories of Suez, which take three hours to get through, even on a good day.

Torque was only one of the problems. Try a few simple angling operations left-handed, with two fingers of the right hand strapped together, and see how far you get. Putting the rod together wasn't too bad, nor was threading the line. But tying the loops and putting on the shot would have baffled Ali Bongo. (Ali Bongo: there's a name to conjure with...)

Then came the really messy bits. I'd bought a fresh tin of maggies, guessing rightly that those left with the landlord would be now severely *hors de combat*. Off came the lid and – whoops! – out came the maggots, all over the bank. It's hard enough retrieving speeding maggies with both hands; with only the left, I didn't nab more than one in three.

Casting was definitely a left-handed job, and it's amazing the difference it makes to your distance and accuracy.

'I couldn't get to within six feet of the spot I wanted,' I confessed to Mad Mac later.

'So what?' he said. 'You never could.'

Ta.

One discovery that I made was that my tobacco consumption doubled. It wasn't that I was smoking the stuff, just that it fell out all over the place whenever I tried to light my pipe. It wasn't difficult to recover it from a pub table, but it was almost impossible to collect it from the bank without the inclusion of one or more foreign bodies. Once you've smoked a few squashed maggots, bits of cheese and selected dried cowpat, you tend to think, 'Blow the expense'.

There were other handicaps, too, of a more personal nature. The kind of thing it's difficult even to torque about. (See how it gets you?)

I couldn't leave the afflicted appendage out in the cold, because the chill went right through to the poor old busted bone. Nor could I put my right mitten on, because the two strapped-up fingers wouldn't go through one hole. So it had to stay stuffed in my pocket or stuck up my jumper.

Scratching. It's amazing the amount of unconscious

scratching you do on the bank: some of it out of boredom; some because of your cramped position, ticklish underwear and wicker-indented backside; some of it because of the flying and crawling creatures which, even in winter, seek refuge on your person.

When you're limited to scratching with the left hand, an amazing amount of your body surface becomes a no-go area for counter-irritation techniques unless you've got an A-level in yoga.

I won't go into left-handed nose-picking, because it could be upsetting for persons of a sensitive disposition. But it's not easy, believe me.

Unshipping the gear at the best of times takes more effort than putting it together. With one hand feeling like a sackful of chisels at the slighest exertion, it's near impossible.

Oh, the shame at having to ask a passing fellow piscator if he'd mind unshipping the bottom joint for me.

'Not at all,' he said, spoiling it with a smirk. 'What's up – afraid you'll never play the violin again?'

Har. Har bloody har.

Back in the pub, fishing for change in left-hand pocket.

'Don't worry,' said the landlord. 'You're in credit. I found out when I checked the slate that I'd charged twice for three pints. There'd been some confusion between your little mate and the barmaid.'

'Sounds like par for the course,' I said. 'So I'm good for three pints, eh?'

'No,' said the landlord. 'Your little mate was in here a minute ago, and he's supped two of them. Said you wouldn't mind.'

'Where is he now?'

'Seems to have slipped out the back way. Funny you didn't see him: it was just as you walked in.'

'Look after the pint for me,' I said. 'I won't be long.'

There are some things you *can* do almost as well with your left hand. And strangling Mad Mac is one of them.

*EVERYTHING YOU NEED TO KNOW ABOUT SPORT
(AND A LOT OF THINGS YOU DON'T)!*

The Book Of

SPORTS
LISTS

CRAIG AND DAVID BROWN

Who 'floats like a butterfly and stings like one too'?
Who gave up sex for a year in order to improve his game
– and what does it cost to persuade John McEnroe to
play with your racquets for a year? Which sportsman
said 'I'd give my right arm to be a pianist' – and what do
Torvill and Dean have to say about each other?

THE BOOK OF SPORTS LISTS brings together the
most remarkable things ever done and the funniest
things ever said in the name of sport around the world.
Record-breakers and blunderers, prudes and Casanovas,
good sports and bad sports, they're all in THE BOOK OF
SPORTS LISTS.

NON-FICTION/HUMOUR/SPORT   0 7221 1935 6   £2.50

*Don't miss Craig Brown and Lesley Cunliffe's THE
BOOK OF ROYAL LISTS, also available in Sphere
Books.*

VIV RICHARDS

The Authorised Biography

TREVOR McDONALD

Viv Richards is not only the world's greatest batsman – he can also be cricket's most entertaining player. Arrogant – wielding his bat in the middle – Viv Richards can also be generous about his opponents, perceptive about his colleagues and self-effacing about his own ability or his magnificent star-studded record.

Today, Richards is recognised as the embodiment of spirit and flair with which the West Indians have always played cricket. However, not since Don Bradman or Gary Sobers has a single player had such an influence on the game. Newscaster and cricket expert Trevor McDonald recounts the peaks and troughs of Richards' career as a Test Cricket and Somerset County player, but above all analyses how both Richards' personality and his game were shaped by the politics and attitudes of the West Indies.

'It is McDonald's particular triumph that he paints Richards upon a canvas that includes the tiny island of his birth . . . helps us to understand the man who has dominated cricket for a decade.' SUNDAY TIMES.

'Here is a biography to match a Richards' innings – thoroughly enjoyable.' SOMERSET COUNTY GAZETTE.

SPORT/BIOGRAPHY   0 7221 5727 4   £1.95

A selection of bestsellers from SPHERE

FICTION

TOUGH GUYS DON'T DANCE	Norman Mailer	£2.50 □
FIRE IN THE ICE	Alan Scholefield	£2.25 □
SOUVENIR	David Kaufelt	£2.50 □
WHAT NIALL SAW	Brian Cullen	£1.25 □
POSSESSIONS	Judith Michael	£2.95 □

FILM & TV TIE-INS

MOG	Peter Tinniswood	£1.95 □
LADY JANE	A. C. H. Smith	£1.95 □
IF I WERE KING OF THE UNIVERSE	Danny Abelson	£1.50 □
BEST FRIENDS	Jocelyn Stevenson	£1.50 □

NON-FICTION

WEEK ENDING: THE CABINET LEAKS	Ian Brown and James Hendrie	£2.95 □
THE POLITICS OF CONSENT	Francis Pym	£2.95 □
THE SPHERE ILLUSTRATED HISTORY OF BRITAIN VOLUMES 1, 2 AND 3	Ed. Kenneth O. Morgan	£3.95 each □

All Sphere books are available at your local bookshop or newsagent, or can be ordered direct from the publisher. Just tick the titles you want and fill in the form below.

Name _____

Address _____

_____

Write to Sphere Books, Cash Sales Department, P.O. Box 11, Falmouth, Cornwall TR10 9EN.

Please enclose a cheque or postal order to the value of the cover price plus:

UK: 55p for the first book, 22p for the second book and 14p for each additional book ordered to a maximum charge of £1.75.

OVERSEAS: £1.00 for the first book plus 25p per copy for each additional book.

BFPO & EIRE: 55p for the first book, 22p for the second book plus 14p per copy for the next 7 books, thereafter 8p per book.

Sphere Books reserve the right to show new retail prices on covers which may differ from those previously advertised in the text or elsewhere, and to increase postal rates in accordance with the PO.